To Mom,

Happy Reading!

Love

Gram

The FRIENDSHIP BOOK

of Francis Gay

D. C. THOMSON & CO. LTD.
London Glasgow Manchester Dundee

A Thought
For Each Day
In 1982

" No man is useless while he has a friend."

Robert Louis Stevenson.

A VILLAGE SPRING

JANUARY

HOW better to start the New Year than by looking at the calendar? It was the late William Barclay, the writer and lecturer, who said that, if he were to be cast up on a desert island, he would like to take with him not a book but a calendar. His point was that whereas every book comes to an end, a calendar gives us a never-ending supply of memories and of hopes.

I am not suggesting that starting a new year is like being cast away on a desert island! But what better equipment could we have as we enter a new year, than good memories of the past and great hopes for the future:

> *" Thankful for all that has been*
> *And trustful for all that's to come."*

A WRITER in a gardening magazine told how he was looking at some motor lawnmowers in a garden centre and on one of them was a notice which read, " If all else fails, please read the instructions!"

If we are honest with ourselves what a lot goes wrong with our lives simply because we try to make things go our way instead of the way in which they were intended. Moral standards, religious ideals, health rules, social obligations, professional integrity—these are but a few of the ways in which we are invited to " read the instructions," and so to find life working for us as it should.

SUNDAY—JANUARY 3.

B E ye angry, and sin not: let not the sun go down upon your wrath.

MONDAY—JANUARY 4.

A FRIEND of ours *almost* got a large bar of milk chocolate as one of his Christmas presents this year. I say " almost " because his four-year-old daughter ate it at five o'clock on Christmas morning. As she quite innocently explained afterwards . . . " I just *had* to eat it, Daddy—I couldn't sleep for worrying, in case it melted!"

TUESDAY—JANUARY 5.

O N January 5, 1922, died one of Britain's most courageous explorers, who had eight years earlier placed this advertisement in the papers:

" Men Wanted for hazardous journey. Small wages, bitter cold, months of complete darkness, constant danger, safe return doubtful. Honour and recognition in case of success."

As a result of that advertisement, Ernest Henry Shackleton had over five thousand applications to sift through. He made four trans-Antarctic journeys, experiencing many adventures, although he never actually reached the South Pole.

On one occasion, as he and two companions struggled over the slippery slopes of South Georgia, he had a strange feeling that there were four, not three of them; and one of his companions later said the same thing. Haven't we all sensed, at some time, an unseen companion by our side? You don't have to go to the ends of the earth to experience it, for He is with us, always.

IT was a cold morning. Faces were long and there was not a smile to be seen in the queue at the baker's.

Then a young coloured man, obviously a newcomer to this country, asked in faltering English for a meat pie.

" Yes," said the assistant. " Cold or warm?"

The young man looked uncertain. Then, rather timidly—" How much is the pie with warmth?" he asked.

As smiles and chuckles broke out around him, the assistant laughed, too. " That's all right, love," she said. " We don't charge for a little warmth!"

IN 1772 the great composer Franz Joseph Haydn and his orchestra were employed by Prince Esterhazy of Hungary. The players had been away from home for many months and they pleaded with Haydn to find some way of asking the autocratic prince for his permission to return to see their families.

So Haydn wrote a special symphony, his 45th, in the final minutes of which he arranged for the players, one by one, to pack up their instruments, blow out their candles and leave the stage. At the end two violinists, including Haydn himself, were all that remained of the orchestra. It is said that Prince Esterhazy laughingly took the hint and gave the orchestra leave of absence the very next day.

I like this story of what is now known as " The Farewell Symphony." In writing it Haydn taught us all a lesson in how to handle an awkward problem with tact and good humour.

HIGH HOPES

" Water the plants," said Daddy,
    " And then you can watch them grow."
Well, I've done just like he told me
    —But my, aren't they slow!

THE FRIENDSHIP BOOK

I'VE got just a little minute,
Only sixty seconds in it,
Forced upon me, can't refuse it,
Didn't seek it, didn't choose it,
But it's up to me to use it.
I must suffer if I lose it,
Give account if I abuse it,
Just a tiny little minute,
But Eternity is in it.

THERE are certain hymns which have a special meaning for all of us. A Scottish minister, the Rev. John Skinner, has told what a certain old psalm means to him. It reminds him how, at the height of the London blitz, he had been listening to the shriek and crash of bombs. Suddenly the noise had ceased and in the silence he heard over the radio, a choir singing:

The Lord of heaven confess,
On high his glory raise.
Him let all angels bless,
Him all his armies praise . . .

For a moment his thoughts had turned from the horrors of war to eternal things. Almost at once the bombs had begun to fall again and the sound of the choir was silenced, but the memory of that wonderful feeling of peace and tranquillity has remained with Mr Skinner to this day.

UNTO every one of us is given grace according to the measure of the gift of Christ.

Monday—January 11.

IN January, 1970, Gladys Aylward died at the age of 68 on the island of Taiwan.

A few weeks earlier one of the orphans she had brought up on the Chinese mainland visited her and asked what she wanted for a Christmas gift. She said she would like a cotton quilt. But when the thermometer dropped to 40° below freezing point, she gave her new quilt to an orphan and her mattress to her Chinese housemaid.

When she died, all that she had was one worn-out blanket. She had given everything else away.

Tuesday—January 12.

THE Lady of the House and I had young married friends to dinner and the conversation turned to the subject of shopping. The young wife said she loved shopping—under two conditions: Firstly, she wanted to be on her own; and secondly she wanted a full purse! But she confessed that these conditions were rarely fulfilled. Either she was accompanied by her husband, striding ahead impatiently while she wanted to look into shop windows; or she had the children with her who insisted on lingering at windows in which she had no interest. And, of course, her purse was never full!

But then, our friend was just experiencing life—where conditions never are ideal. Long ago, a Bible writer said, " He that observeth the wind shall not sow; and he that regardeth the clouds shall not reap." If we wait for the ideal time for any enterprise, we shall wait for ever. It's when we determine to make the best of things, that conditions don't seem to be so bad after all.

UNDERSTANDING

The young and the old can be excellent friends
　　With notions and views to exchange;
Though looking at life from opposite ends,
　　They do not consider it strange;
In fact if you listen you'll find they agree
On matters the rest of us don't even see!

SOME schoolchildren were asked to give a definition of what Life is. Not an easy thing to do at any age, but I think that three little Pakistani children, aged 8, 10 and 12, made a pretty good stab at it. Here is some of what they wrote:

> *Life is Precious—Guard it;*
> *Life is a Challenge—Meet it;*
> *Life is Tense—Ease it;*
> *Life is Sweet—Taste it;*
> *Life is Love—Kiss it;*
> *Life is Promise—Keep it;*
> *Life is God—Worship it;*
> *Life is Pleasure—Enjoy it;*
> *Life is Rough—Smooth it;*
> *Life is Duty—Do it;*
> *Life is Life—Live it!*

THURSDAY—JANUARY 14.

A GERMAN story from the 14th century tells of an old woman who was once found in the streets of Strasbourg carrying a bucket of water in one hand and a flaming torch in the other. When asked what she was going to do she said that with the water she was going to put out the flames of hell, and with the torch she was going to burn up heaven. Why? So that men and women would love God for Himself alone and not from fear of punishment or desire for reward.

If we are honest with ourselves we must admit that our motives for our good deeds are often mixed. Only love, true, deep love for someone or something beyond ourselves, can cleanse our motives and give meaning to our lives.

B

THOMAS GUY was one of London's most prosperous citizens in 1666. He could have lived in comfort and luxury. Instead, this shabbily dressed man shared his wealth with those who were sick and destitute as a result of the Great Fire which had just ravaged London.

It would have been easy to hand his money out to charitable causes for others to distribute, but that was not his way. Instead, he took the trouble to find out about individual cases of need and then arranged for personal help to be given.

His gifts were always anonymous and during his lifetime few people knew about his generosity, but since his death, thousands have been grateful for the healing of the famous London hospital which bears his name.

SATURDAY—JANUARY 16.

THE late Earl Mountbatten of Burma was once asked in an interview for BBC Television if he had ever met his great-grandmother, Queen Victoria.

He said, " Well, if you ' meet ' someone at your christening when you're just a baby, then I did. I'm told that she held me on that occasion, and the lady-in-waiting who handed me over to Queen Victoria says I tweaked her nose, and I think I pulled her spectacles off—so I must have known her fairly well!"

Who could have got away with such behaviour to Queen Victoria, without rebuke, except a baby? It was a charming beginning—and Lord Louis went on charming people for the rest of his distinguished life.

THE FRIENDSHIP BOOK

THERE is no fear in love; but perfect love casteth out fear.

IT was eight o'clock on a winter-wet Monday morning, and five-year-old Katie Mitchell was none too keen on getting ready to go to school. There and then she decided on her future career.

" When I'm grown up," she said, " I'm going to be a Mummy."

" Oh, why's that?" her mother asked.

" Because then I'll be able to stay at home in the warm and eat cream buns all day!"

ERIC HOSKING is one of Britain's most accomplished wild-life photographers. He has taken brilliant pictures of creatures of all kinds. But such work is not without risk. One night, when he was quite a young man, he was attacked by a tawny owl, which blinded him in one eye.

Instead of becoming bitter about it, Eric took it cheerfully and philosophically. I think his reaction is a lesson to us all. " She was merely protecting her young," he said. " Anyway, she did me a favour. Everyone else has to close one eye to take a photograph. I don't have to bother!"

After his accident he continued his career, photographing the birds he loved and taking some of the finest wildlife pictures in the world.

With the same sort of attitude, we can use our own set-backs and disasters as a step towards more triumphant living.

LITTLE WORLD

Some folk like bustling cities
—That's where they like to be,
But there's no place quite so friendly
As a town beside the sea.

A SMALL girl had watched part of a war film on television and was obviously disturbed by it. " Mummy," she asked, " Was the war *before* Jesus was born?"

" Why, no dear," was the reply. " It was a long time after. Why do you ask?"

" Well, I didn't think people would want to kill each other after Jesus came."

How that little child's simple faith shames all our peace plans and peace conferences! I remember the words of the poet Francis Thompson, " Know you what it is to be a child? It is to be something very different from a man. It is to believe in love, to believe in loveliness, to believe in belief."

What a difference it would make to us and to our world if we had that childlike spirit.

A NEIGHBOUR rushed up to a Yorkshire farmer with some bad news. He told him that the river had suddenly flooded and carried off all the farmer's pigs.

" What about Farmer Brown's pigs?" he asked. He was told that they also had been carried off by the flood.

" And what about Farmer Smith's?" Yes. They had been lost, too.

" Ah, well," said the farmer. " It's not as bad as I thought, then."

In a strange way he was right. Remember how people gained comfort and strength during the last war when they were all up against it, all in the same boat? Troubles shared are always more easily borne.

I CALLED to see old Mrs Harris who is housebound and lives alone. When she showed me into her sitting-room I noticed two cups and saucers set out on a tray.

Thinking she was expecting another visitor I decided not to stay long and after we had chatted for a while I rose to take my leave.

" Don't go yet," urged Mrs Harris.

" But aren't you expecting someone?" I asked, glancing at the tea tray.

" Oh, I always set tea for two," she explained. " It's just in case someone drops in. So you see, you're my surprise guest for today."

Despite her age and her arthritis Mrs Harris still brews a good pot of tea. I don't know when I enjoyed an afternoon cuppa so much.

Thank you, Mrs Harris!

SATURDAY—JANUARY 23.

DURING the reign of King George V, Belisha Beacons were introduced at pedestrian crossings.

One day, whilst motoring in London with his Queen, His Majesty decided to test these crossings for himself. The chauffeur was ordered to stop, and King George descended.

Moments later he returned, chuckling, and told the Queen, " One of my devoted subjects has just called me a ' doddering old idiot '!"

SUNDAY—JANUARY 24.

BE thou faithful unto death, and I will give thee a crown of life.

THE FRIENDSHIP BOOK

IT'S easy to joke about things that don't matter, but sometimes one's feelings are too deep for lightheartedness. I was very impressed the other evening when listening to an interview. The couple being interviewed had been married for 80 years—yes, 80.

Jokingly, the interviewer said to the wife: " I suppose you got fed up with him sometimes?"

Her simple reply was: " How can you get fed up with somebody you love?"

I READ once that a psychiatrist learned much about his clients' personalities by the way they selected a chocolate from a box. Some chose at random, taking the first chocolate their hand met, others looked carefully at the chocolates themselves before taking one, while others studied the printed key and carefully selected their favourite one.

According to the psychiatrist, random selectors tended to be happy-go-lucky extroverts, while the more careful selectors were often rather inhibited and tended to be introverts.

Believe it if you like. What is certain about a box of assorted chocolates is that the whole world seems to have co-operated in bringing them to you. There are coffee beans from South America, oranges from the Mediterranean, strawberries from England, hazelnuts from Turkey, sugar from the West Indies, almonds from Spain, cocoa beans from West Africa and much more.

It's quite a thought, but when you think of it, you can find the world in a box of chocolates.

WEDNESDAY—JANUARY 27.

ON Sunday, 27th January, 1980, the Rev. Charles Bird celebrated his 100th birthday by preaching from the pulpit in his birthday suit.

This was by no means as unseemly as it might sound. Ten years earlier when Mr Bird was being fitted out for a new suit, he asked the assistant if there was any discount for nonagenarians.

He was told to come back when he was 100 and he would be given a free suit. He did just that—and as his 100th birthday approached, the tailor honoured his promise and presented Mr Bird with his new " birthday suit " which he duly wore in the pulpit.

THURSDAY—JANUARY 28.

A BOY called Eddie Frankland of Rossendale in Lancashire wrote this version of the 23rd Psalm when he was nine years old:

" The Lord is my shepherd, and I am one of His sheep; no matter where He leadeth me I have not got to grumble or find fault—whether it be a rough road or whether it be a nice cool shady field. I have got to remember that wherever I go He will be leading me, and knows what is the best for me; and if I believe in Him and do His works and obey His commands I shall be happy both in body and soul. I have also to remember that in the time of disappointments or even at the time of death—if I own Him as my shepherd He will be there to comfort me as no one else can, and when at last I leave this earth He will guide me into His Heavenly fold, where sorrow, and grief and tears are not known, but where everyone lives happy and contented for evermore."

FRIDAY—JANUARY 29.

TEENAGER Ian Stafford of Sheffield loves helping people, especially those who are handicapped. So when he heard that two-year-old Stephen Walker could not sit up and play without a support, Ian decided to make him one. With help from his school he designed and made a small mobile chair which gave little Stephen the help and support he needed.

When he was praised for what he had done, Ian's simple comment was " I'm glad Stephen likes his chair." A humble and self-effacing remark from a young man who, by the way, is himself a cripple and suffers almost constant pain.

Isn't it true that if you look long enough, you will always find someone worse off than yourself?

SATURDAY—JANUARY 30.

WHEN he was a young shop assistant in charge of a grocery store, Abraham Lincoln once found that he had accidentally overcharged a customer by three cents. As soon as he put up the shutters at closing time, and before going home himself, he walked two miles to the customer's house to repay the three cents.

A simple act, but it was the same honesty and concern for others which he was to bring to his political career and which was to make him the best loved of all American Presidents.

SUNDAY—JANUARY 31.

O MY GOD, I trust in thee: let me not be ashamed, let not mine enemies triumph over me.

FEBRUARY

To make a marriage happy
You need a lot of love
And, added to it, thoughtfulness,
The things you're dreaming of:
Patience, understanding,
Good times and laughter, too,
Mixed in with pride and caring
And sharing all you do.

Do you take your hands for granted?
An unusual question, perhaps. Yet, Mrs Nancy Graham, a housewife in Aberdeen, gave it some thought. She'd had a busy week, almost too busy for one pair of hands, but when she had a few minutes to spare she sat down and dashed off these lines—

Oh, blessings for the gift of hands, hands that can work in many ways; fashion wood, drive cars, lead bands, knit and sew, write books and plays. Hands that can work, hands that can play, hands that can golf and fish and bowl; hands that can cook meals every day, hands that can help a poorer soul.

Hands that can heal, hands soft to touch, hands that can play sweet airs of old; hands stretched to welcome—all are such—hands that are worth their weight in gold. Give me helpful hands for doing good in tasks God meant our hands to do; skilled or unskilled to use as I should, to help those dear—and others, too.

SOON after Diana Pitcher had moved into her Dorset cottage after living in South Africa, she slipped on some black ice and for a time knew no more.

Later it transpired that she had been found lying injured and unconscious by the local milkman. He drove her into Sherborne, waited at the casualty department of the hospital for two hours, and when she was admitted, he went back to her cottage, cleaned up her grate, tidied up generally and, after locking up, had her keys delivered to her in hospital.

When Diana returned home two weeks later, and expressed her heartfelt gratitude to him, this good man's simple reply was, " Well, isn't life for helping people?"

I OFTEN remember my old friend Albert. He knew when he was nearing the end of a long and full life—but he was not at all afraid. " The word ' fear ' is not in my dictionary," he once told me. " I like to think positively, so I prefer *rich* words."

When I asked him for an example of a rich word, he spoke to me about love. " What can be richer than knowing the love of God and giving back a little of it in return?" he said. " And what a rich feeling it is to be kept safe and warm in the love of one's own family, surrounded by the love of lifelong companions."

Yes, Albert was right. Love *is* a rich word. Often, our most valuable possession is love. Yet it's free, it accumulates, and it's burglar-proof!

EUREKA!

What secrets does the test-tube hold
Coaxed forth by magic flame?
Perhaps my experiment will lead
To scientific fame!

FRIDAY—FEBRUARY 5.

THE other evening the Lady of the House and I got talking about marriage. We were trying to work out what makes a happy marriage and, between you and me, we were finding it a tough question to answer. These are some of the things we thought of:

Willingness to adjust to each other; a readiness to compromise; tolerance, laughter, sympathy and forgiveness; the ability to accept each other as he or she is.

I can't remember now which of us remembered something that a writer called Wilbert D. Gough once said, but in a way it says it all:

" In marriage, *being* the right person is as important as *finding* the right person."

SATURDAY—FEBRUARY 6.

I THINK that Dr Samuel Johnson, the great 18th century wit and man of letters, is one of the most quotable men I know. He seemed to be able to say so much in a short, terse sentence. Here is one of his less familiar remarks which I happened to come across the other day. It's straight and to the point: " The habit of looking on the best side is worth more than a thousand pounds a year."

I will just add one small point. In these inflationary times I think he might have said " a hundred thousand pounds a year!"

SUNDAY—FEBRUARY 7.

I WAITED patiently for the Lord; and he inclined unto me, and heard my cry.

G. K. CHESTERTON once said that it saddened him when he heard people express the thought: "The day will soon come when communicating with the distant stars will seem as ordinary a thing as answering a telephone." What he would like to hear them say, he explained, was that, "The day will soon come when answering the telephone will seem to be as wonderful a thing as communicating with the distant stars."

It was a plea not to lose our sense of wonder—something which, in a world of increasing scientific knowledge becomes all too easy. We tend to take marvels for granted and become blasé about them. People used to talk about the Seven Wonders of the World, but the world has always had far more than seven wonders!

Still, seven is a start. How about making a list *now* of seven wonderful things?

TUESDAY—FEBRUARY 9.

BRUNO GIORDANO, the 16th century Italian philosopher, suffered many things for his beliefs and indeed was eventually burned at the stake. In an earlier imprisonment he was taunted by a fellow-prisoner as to whether he could still believe in God. His reply was, "The very straw in my mattress is sufficient proof of God's care for me." I have no doubt that even at his terrible death he was upheld by his faith.

If Giordano could find the assurance of Providence from the straw in his prison mattress, might we not find it too in the many blessings of our liberty?

THE other day a friend in Australia sent me a letter which closed with this very moving wish:

" In the meantime, may the day break, the shadows flee away, and love be always waiting for you at the end of every day."

What a lovely benediction!

MANY years ago, a Methodist minister visited a miner's house in County Durham where the man's wife was ill.

As he entered, he missed his footing and fell down some steps just inside the front door. He turned a somersault, and landed in a sitting position on the kitchen floor in full view of the startled miner and his wife, who was in bed in the room.

The minister rose gingerly and made his way to a chair in the corner. However, in his confusion he did not hear the couple say, " Don't sit on that chair, sir." The chair had only three of its legs, so over he went again—and this time knocked over a flour-bin so that he was covered with flour.

The miner and his wife roared with laughter, and the minister also tried to laugh as well.

Some weeks later he called again at the house. " How is Mrs. Hammerton today?"

" Oh," beamed the miner, " she is quite well now; your visit did her good."

She had been suffering from a quinsy in her throat. She had laughed so much that the quinsy had burst, and she got well again almost at once.

It's an ill wind!

FRIDAY—FEBRUARY 12.

WHEN little Tom's grandmother died his mother wasn't sure how she should best break the news to him. That night when they were having tea together she said, " Tom, I've got some sad news to tell you. We won't be seeing Granny any more."

" Oh," said Tom. " Why's that?"

His mother fidgeted uneasily.

" Well Tom," she said, " she's gone to live with God."

" Crumbs," said Tom. " How posh!"

SATURDAY—FEBRUARY 13.

IF you hold your hand in front of your eyes it will hide from your gaze even the tallest mountain. I use this simple illustration to remind you that the world is full of wonder and beauty which we often fail to see simply because we let our busy lives or anxieties get in the way of it.

This is why we need some time each day to relax and why we need holidays. Not just for the sake of relaxation, but to give us time to enjoy the simple things of life which make the world wonderful—all that grows, the laughter of people, the sound of children playing, the shapes of the clouds and countless things which may not find mention in the glossy holiday brochures, simply because the best things in life *are* free!

SUNDAY—FEBRUARY 14.

SURELY goodness and mercy shall follow me all the days of my life: and I will dwell in the house of the Lord for ever.

O NE of the nice things about being in the depths of winter is that we are tempted to sit by our firesides and read books about foreign places where the climate is even colder, so by contrast the weather doesn't seem too bad. On one such evening recently I was reading about penguins on the Antarctic ice-cap. Apparently they *need* to be extra sociable, otherwise they'd freeze to death in the terrible, bitter, gale-force winds. Standing in a group, they huddle together to generate warmth, and in this way the stronger members are able to share in a real sense with the elderly or weak members among them.

Are we so very different when it comes to needing a bit of the warmth of human friendship? Don't we all need that daily dose of human contact? There are times when our friends are an essential part of our survival kit. And there are times when we are a part of theirs.

TUESDAY—FEBRUARY 16.

I N Robert Bolt's very successful play and film *A Man For All Seasons*, the main character, Thomas More, gives a young man this advice:

" Why not be a teacher?" he says. " You'd be a fine teacher. Perhaps a great one."

The young man is not impressed. " And if I was, who would know?" he asks.

Thomas More tells him, " You, your pupils, your friends, God. Not a bad public that."

It's very much the same public that recognises and appreciates the qualities of a mother or father, wife or husband, aunt or uncle or the qualities of a friend. Not a bad public at all.

C

WEDNESDAY—FEBRUARY 17.

I HAVE always admired the Red Indians for their traditional code of conduct and their profound wisdom. Take this prayer, for instance, which they used to offer to the Great Spirit:

" Grant that I may not criticise my neighbours until I have walked a mile in his moccasins."

We would all do well, at times, to remember that thought.

THURSDAY—FEBRUARY 18.

EMPTY vessels make the most noise," they say, and Mr Talkative got a bad write-up in John Bunyan's *Pilgrim's Progress*. Yet the world would be a poorer place if everyone was the silent type.

Some talkative people can be bores, but the chatterers of this world are often those who are interested in a great variety of things. They are often more generous than others because of their outgoing nature.

The chief trouble with talkative people is that they *will* interrupt—but then the person who never interrupts probably isn't really listening to you!

FRIDAY—FEBRUARY 19.

IF you've made a mess of things—
Much that you regret;
If your heart is grieved because
Of things you can't forget;
Look forward to tomorrow,
Don't yesterday deplore—
With a bit of faith and pluck,
Begin again once more!

SATURDAY—FEBRUARY 20.

THE other day I was shown a little magazine published by the organisation Age Concern and I was greatly taken with these words written by an unknown Mum.

" My son said one day: ' I don't know why I don't like school because, really, I quite enjoy it.' As I washed the dishes I thought how true this is. I don't know why I don't like washing dishes because really, I quite enjoy it.

" It is the thought we dislike, the deed we quite enjoy. Sometimes we have to force ourselves to get up and go out, to talk to people, to cook a meal—the list seems endless and yet, when we think of it later, we realise that we did enjoy it and it was worth the effort."

SUNDAY—FEBRUARY 21.

I WILL give unto him that is athirst of the fountain of the water of life freely.

MONDAY—FEBRUARY 22.

ELSIE came home from school one day and said proudly, " I know all my tables—even the twelve times." Teasingly, her grandpa asked, " What is thirteen times thirteen?"

Scornfully came the reply, " Don't be silly, Grandpa. There's no such thing!"

But if that little girl's knowledge was limited, so is that of us all. People who " think they know it all " rob themselves of a very great deal of life's satisfaction. On the tomb of a great scholar was the epitaph, " He died learning ". When we stop learning there is a sense in which we stop living.

HOW much do you rely on first impressions?
A lot? Then I wonder what you'd have made of William Wilberforce. Always a delicate child, he reached manhood undersized, pale and weak, but inside that tiny frame beat a lion's heart.

His speeches were passionate in defence of the downtrodden. One observer remarked—" I saw what seemed a mere shrimp of a man mounted upon the table, but as I listened, he grew and grew until the shrimp became a whale."

His health got worse, and on doctor's orders he took some opium every day to keep body and soul together, yet he had the tremendous willpower never to increase the dose. Despite repeated disappointments over a score of years, he did more than any other person to stop the slave trade.

The point I want to make is this. If he had been a handsome, brawny man enjoying robust health, would the world ever have heard of him? I doubt it. It was his sensitive, suffering life which shaped his unconquerable sympathy for the oppressed.

When you're tempted to make a snap judgment, remember William Wilberforce and first impressions.

WE all of us hear bits of gossip from time to time. How should we react? I think we should ask ourselves, " Is it kind? Is it true? Is it necessary? " My experience is that gossip never stands up to these three searching questions! And even if it fails only one of them, then the best thing to do is to forget what we have heard as quickly as possible.

THE FRIENDSHIP BOOK

FRED was born in Alliston, Ontario, in 1891. When he was a teenager he had a school friend called Jane who became ill with a mystery disease. Within a few months she was dead.

That could have been the end of the story, but the young girl's tragic death made such an impression on Fred that he vowed he would conquer the disease we now know as diabetes. Perhaps you know his second name—Banting. Along with Charles Best he toiled away until they had learnt how to prepare insulin and so save untold millions of lives, which would otherwise have been lost through diabetes.

A good illustration of the fact that when we react to misfortune in a positive way tremendous good can come out of evil. Thanks to the work of Banting and Best, countless diabetics—and amongst them could be you or one of your friends—are now able to lead full and healthy lives.

THE seaside town of Lowestoft is the most easterly point in England. Local people claim that when the sun rises, the first object in Great Britain to catch the light of the morning sun is the golden weathercock on top of the steeple of St Margaret's church.

Holidaymakers look up hopefully for clear skies and the warm sun. And the sun *is* there—although sometimes hidden by clouds.

When you think about it, friendship is a bit like that—the important thing is not to be always bright and shiny, but simply to be there. That is enough.

HAVE A HEART!

My master's paper's not much fun,
    The football page, a bore.
I hope he'll take me for a run
    When he has found the score!

WHEN John Smeaton, the Yorkshire engineer, was invited to build a lighthouse on the notorious Eddystone Rock 14 miles off Plymouth, he faced a tremendous challenge. Two previous lighthouses had met with disaster. Both were built of wood and the first, Winstanley's, was swept away by a storm in 1704. The second, built by John Rudyard, was destroyed by a fire started by the lighthouse's own candles.

Smeaton was convinced that the only solution was to build it with granite blocks, dovetailed together. This suggestion was met with great scepticism from those who were employing him. The argument of both Winstanley and Rudyard had been that a wooden tower would have a certain flexibility when it met the force of the gales. A solid stone tower would not seem to have that capacity.

" Surely," Smeaton was asked, " when the tower meets the force of the storm, something must give way?"

" Certainly," was his reply. " The storm must give way!"

So, in life, there are those who think that the storms should have the last word, but there are others, like Smeaton, who believe that storms are to be withstood.

Someone was once asked, " Well, how is life using you?" The reply was, " That is the wrong question. You ought to ask how am I using life?"

SUNDAY—FEBRUARY 28.

BUT the meek shall inherit the earth; and shall delight themselves in the abundance of peace.

MARCH

DURING the last war a padre was talking to a soldier—a tough, hard-drinking type who didn't wear his heart on his sleeve, yet whom the padre suspected came from a God-fearing family. The soldier asked, " Padre, can you tell me how it is that sometimes when my nerves are all a-twitter, I suddenly feel calm and ready for anything ?"

The padre paused for a moment and then said, " Might it not be that your mother is praying for you ?"

The man's face suddenly softened and his eyes shone. " Padre, you may be right. It's just the sort of thing my mother would be doing !"

How much there may be happening in our lives because others are praying for us ! How much may happen in others' lives because we are praying for them !

SOME people, men as well as women, don't like being asked their age. But a friend of mine takes great delight in answering the question. Someone asked him the other day. " I'm 71 years *young*," he answered with pride in his voice.

It reminded me of the remark once made by Sir William Beveridge, one of the pioneers of the Welfare State. " Some people are born about 65 years old and are always ready to retire. Some stay 21 until they are 90."

How true it is that age is more a state of mind than a measurement in years.

THE FRIENDSHIP BOOK

LITTER still remains a big problem in our towns and cities. Some even go so far as to have a slogan on litter-bins stating: " The tidiness of our town depends on YOU." This is true, for many people leave tidiness to others. They think, " Oh, it doesn't matter what I do."

Perhaps they should be reminded of the king who ordered all the people in his capital city to take a jug of milk and pour it into a certain fountain. The fountain would then flow with free milk for poor people and beggars.

The idea was first class, but first one person and then others decided that it would not matter if they took water—there would be so much milk taken by other people that it would make no difference. But it did—for when the fountain flowed, it consisted of very weak milky water! The king's scheme was ruined.

WHEN the woodruff blooms,
When the butterfly takes wing,
When the bumble-bee hums,
Then it's Spring.

When the cuckoo calls,
When the pipit starts to sing,
When the meadow glows green,
Then it's Spring.

When the mayflies dance,
When the kestrel acts as king,
When the whole world smiles,
Then it's Spring!

FRIDAY—MARCH 5.

I ALWAYS pay special attention when I am talking to a keen gardener. In their own quiet way they have a lot to say that is well worth listening to.

A friend was telling me about an old gardener who has a border of polyanthus, the little multi-coloured flowers which make such a splash of brightness. One day my friend asked him why he kept so many of a very plain, pale yellow strain, when he could so easily replace them.

The gardener smiled. " It's the plain ones which set the rest off," he explained.

You see what I mean?

SATURDAY—MARCH 6.

ARE you a generous person? Not just with money, but with time, thoughtfulness and consideration.

There are some folk who find sympathising with other peoples' troubles quite easy. Yet they find it hard to rejoice with them in their happiness. Just let those unfortunates have a stroke of good fortune and see how quickly some folk are jealous of them! Their generosity immediately dries up.

There is an old story of a Spaniard who always put on his spectacles when he was eating cherries. He said they seemed much larger that way. It is the same with us. If we put on our generous spectacles to look at people, their good qualities will stand out and be more noticeable.

SUNDAY—MARCH 7.

BEHOLD, I stand at the door, and knock.

DR. JAMES DOBSON was until 1963 a science teacher at Cedarlane Junior High School in Los Angeles. He believed strongly in both kindness and firm discipline, and rarely had any trouble with his students.

Twelve years after he had left he had a phone call from a girl called Julie whom he had not seen or heard from since she had been a pupil in his science class. After some moments chatting, she asked him which church he attended. Dr. Dobson told her, and she then asked if she could come along some Sunday morning.

Julie came, came again, and in due course found out what it was to be a real Christian. She joined the choir, and every time she sang, a radiant glow appeared on her face.

Some time afterwards Dr. Dobson asked her why she had telephoned him twelve years after he had left her school and why she had asked what church he attended.

Julie answered simply: " Because when I was in my second year at school, you were the only person in my whole life who acted like you respected and believed in me . . . and I wanted to know your God."

TUESDAY—MARCH 9.

THE CHURCH GARDEN

FIRST plant two rows of PEAS: Prayer and Perseverance.

Then plant two rows of LETTUCE: Let us be faithful, and Let us follow Christ.

Then plant two rows of TURNIPS: Turn up for church, and Turn up with a smile.

THE FRIENDSHIP BOOK

A YOUNG poet approached an editor with a batch of poems which he hoped might be published.

" What are they about?" asked the editor.

" They are about love," replied the poet.

" I see," said the editor. " And what is love?"

The poet at once launched into a lyrical account of moonlight and roses and soft music and all the rest of it, but the editor shook his head and stopped him.

" Nonsense!" he said. " Love is about getting up in the middle of a cold winter's night to fill hot water bottles for ailing children!"

How much nearer the truth he was than the poet! Love is not just an emotion, but an activity. Our love finds its fullest expression in what we can do for others to help and encourage, to comfort and heal.

O NE teacher in my schooldays I always remember, not because he was particularly good at teaching his subject, but for the little bits of wisdom he slipped into our lessons. Once he was explaining how the scientist Galileo discovered that the earth revolved round the sun and not the sun round the earth.

" This was an important discovery," he said. " But an even more important discovery we all need to make is that the world does not revolve around us."

There were better teachers at our school than that man, but do you wonder that I still remember and treasure many of the wise things he said?

FRIDAY—MARCH 12.

IT was the legendary Josh Billings who wrote the following lines:

So many Gods, so many creeds,
So many paths that wind and wind;
While just the act of being kind
Is all this sad world needs.

SATURDAY—MARCH 13.

A DOCTOR friend of mine, whom I shall call Clive, was digging his garden one day when a little fair head pushed its way through the hedge which divides his house from the one next door. David, aged two, and Clive, aged forty-two, introduced themselves, and at once became firm friends.

As David grew up, Clive took him sailing, and for long tramps in the hills. Now, David is a man himself, and a surgeon. When I heard about this friendship I thought of an endearing story I had read about the writer, John Buchan, Lord Tweedsmuir. He, too, was able to help the son of one of his close friends. He was grateful, he said, for the opportunity of sharing his experience with a younger man.

We cannot all be as good a companion and doctor as Clive, or as accomplished as John Buchan, but, with thought, we can all devote time and energy to starting off a youngster on the right lines.

SUNDAY—MARCH 14.

SING unto the Lord a new song; play skilfully with a loud noise.

COURAGE

*Life's obstacles can fill the mind
If overmuch we fear them;
Attacked with boldness we may find
How easily we clear them.*

MONDAY—MARCH 15.

IN his best-selling book, *Watership Down,* Robert Adams writes, " When Marco Polo came at last to Cathay, seven hundred years ago, did he not feel—and did not his heart falter as he realised—that this great and splendid capital of an empire had had its being all the years of his life and far longer, and that he had been ignorant of it? ... That it was full of wonders beyond his understanding? That his arrival was of no importance whatever? ... There is nothing that cuts you down to size like coming to some strange and marvellous place where no-one even stops to notice that you stare about you."

It would be tragic if, in this world of ever-increasing wonders, we should come to take them all for granted, and lose our sense of wonder. But if we really go about with our eyes open, our ears alert, our spirits and minds sensitive, then there is little fear of that.

Let's see how many wonders we can encounter today!

TUESDAY—MARCH 16.

A YOUNG church member about to set off to a holiday conference was busily packing his bag.

" Are you nearly ready?" called his mother.

" Yes, I won't be long," he answered. " I have just to put in a guide book, a mirror, a lamp, a telescope, a microscope, some history and poetry books, a bundle of old letters, a sword, a hammer, and a suit of armour."

And he placed his Bible in his case and closed the lid.

WEDNESDAY—MARCH 17.

THERE was a friendly enmity between these two great men George Bernard Shaw and Winston Churchill. One day, Shaw wrote to Churchill, " Here are two tickets for my new play. Bring a friend—if you have one."

And Churchill sent back a note saying, " Sorry, I can't make the first night, but I'll be happy to come to the second—if there is one."

THURSDAY—MARCH 18.

OVER 200 years ago a certain John Burton posed an unusual question and gave a surprising answer. " Why is it," he asked, " that the oxen, the swine, the women and all other creatures are so long-legged in Sussex?"

And his explanation? " May it be from the difficulty of pulling the feet out of so much mud by the strength of the ankles that the muscles get stretched, as it were, and the bones lengthened?"

Well, I don't know about pulling out the feet, but I have a feeling that John Burton may have been quietly pulling our legs! All the same, how true it is that struggle and not ease, effort, not idleness, are the qualities which strengthen our spirits.

FRIDAY—MARCH 19.

SORRY, I haven't got a minute to spare!" Don't let yourself get into the habit of saying that. You might come to believe it. And your friends, being sympathetic, will believe it, too. Until, in the end, you'll have far too many spare minutes—and all of them empty.

ONE spring morning a newly-hatched swallow was seen to fall to the ground from the eaves of a bungalow. It tried desperately to walk on the grass and use its wings.

The parents swooped and circled around their little one as if trying to encourage it. When the baby made a supreme effort and began to climb the thick trunk of a tree, his parents would pass so near it was as if they were trying to hold him up in case he started to fall. Time after time they came and went while their baby continued working with his wings until he could fly on his own.

Isn't that the best kind of attitude we parents should take to our children? Love them, encourage them, challenge them as they go through new experiences on their own—learning to fledge their own wings in life?

HE that loveth not knoweth not God; for God is love.

FIVE-YEAR-OLD Jamie was doing his best to remember a lesson in manners. " Always say something nice to people, and pay them a compliment when you can," his mother had told him.

So, when Jamie found himself standing next to a very overweight lady in the library, he racked his brain for something to say. Then he declared, in loud, ringing tones, " Hello, you're definitely the thinnest fat lady I have ever seen!"

D

TUESDAY—MARCH 23.

HAVE you heard about the young man who spent a long time searching for the perfect wife? Eventually he found her. But unfortunately it didn't lead to anything. The trouble was that *she* was looking for the perfect husband!

Personally, I think " perfect " people would be rather boring and difficult to live with, don't you?

WEDNESDAY—MARCH 24.

DO you know these lovely lines by an unknown hand? They are entitled " My Beatitude ", and I saw them hanging recently in an old folks' home. Whoever wrote them spoke for old folk everywhere:

Blessed are they who understand my faltering step
*   and palsied hand;*
Blessed who know my ears today must strain to
*   catch the things they say;*
Blessed are they who seem to know that my eyes
*   are dim and my wits are slow;*
Blessed are they who looked away when coffee
*   spilled at the table today;*
Blessed are they with cheery smile who stop to
*   chat for a little while;*
Blessed are they who never say, " You told that
*   story twice today ";*
Blessed are they who know the ways to bring back
*   memories of yesterdays;*
Blessed are they who make it known that I'm
*   loved, respected, and not alone;*
Blessed who know I'm at a loss to find more
*   strength to bear my cross;*
Blessed are they who ease the days on my
*   journey home in loving ways.*

ONE of the hardest questions of all to answer at a time of tragedy is: " Why does God let this happen?"

A missionary friend once told me of a Chinese parable. In it, he said, life is likened to an intricate piece of embroidery. From the back, it's a meaningless mass of tangled threads with no apparent design. But on the other side there's the perfect pattern of the embroidery with not a stitch out of place.

So it is, said the missionary, with life and death. Here we see just part of the pattern—the chaotic tangle. Only when we pass to the other side will it be revealed how all things work together in a flawless design.

It's a parable that can bring comfort in the midst of distress.

DR. DAVID SMITH, scholar, author and preacher, has told how, during his boyhood in the West of Scotland, he and a friend made a huge kite, but when they tried to fly it, it kept swooping down to earth. An old fisherman who was watching them told them to tie a divot—a turf—to its tail, and when they had done this their kite flew beautifully, though secretly they had expected that the divot would hold *down* the kite, not help it to rise.

How often it is the things we would count as heavy and burdensome which in fact can lift us up in faith and hope:

" Still by my woes to be
Nearer my God to Thee."

SATURDAY—MARCH 27.

WHAT a lot we can often learn from people who seem to have suffered more than their share of hardship and loss. An old friend was left a widow with several young children. Her husband had been ill for some time before his death and unable to work, so her material resources were slender. But throughout this difficult period she maintained a cheerful and courageous outlook, and sometimes she would recall words which she said her grandmother had used in very similar circumstances: " He who loses wealth, loses much, and he who loses a friend, loses more. But he who loses faith, loses all."

It may be faith in ourselves, in our work, in the future, in other people, in God—but without *some* faith we are poor indeed.

SUNDAY—MARCH 28.

AND be ye kind one to another, tenderhearted, forgiving one another, even as God for Christ's sake hath forgiven you.

MONDAY—MARCH 29.

SOMEBODY said something really nice to me today—a friendly compliment, and it seemed absolutely sincere. What was said doesn't really matter, but I know it sent me on my way feeling so much happier. And it reminded me of that old Chinese proverb: " A kind word will keep you warm for three winters."

If you have any kind words to bestow, don't hold them back. Remember, it's warmth you're spreading.

TUESDAY—MARCH 30.

I HAVE forgotten most of what my mathematics teacher taught me at school, except this small but useful piece of advice:

"When you face life's problems, do so from this angle—the *Try Angle.*"

WEDNESDAY—MARCH 31.

WHEN the Rev. Sabine Baring-Gould, author of the hymn, "Onward Christian Soldiers", was rector of the North Devon church at Lewtrenchard, where he ministered for over forty years, he used to delight in taking visitors round the church and churchyard and pointing out to them the things of special interest.

He never failed to show them the tomb of a predecessor of his, of many years before, which was set just inside the churchyard wall. The tombstone had been erected by grateful members of the parish and it listed the ways in which the rector had faithfully fulfilled his ministry.

When Baring-Gould asked visitors if they noticed anything unusual about the stone the more observant would remark, "Why, yes! There is no name on it! Who was he?"

"That's the point," said the rector. "Generations of schoolboys have sat on the bank above the stone, and their feet have gradually worn away the inscription of the name on the top line. So, we don't know who he was, only what he did!"

People may not remember *who* we are, but if there is some piece of service, some word of encouragement, some deed of mercy that we have contributed to their lives, that is our true memorial.

ORPHANS

Blessed are they
Who from the storm
Save little lives
And keep them warm.

APRIL

THURSDAY—APRIL 1.

WILL anybody make an April Fool of you today? Nobody really knows how the custom started, but it seems to be at least as old as the Romans, and may be connected with the comic pagan god Lud, from whose name the word " ludicrous " is said to have come.

I think April Fool's Day is a pleasant and harmless tradition. Some of our humour today is based on cruel satire, often in bad taste. But a bit of innocent fun is one of the ways of keeping ourselves cheerful. So if somebody pulls your leg today, take it in good part!

FRIDAY—APRIL 2.

WHEN 18-year-old Peter Everett of Aigburth, Liverpool, collapsed and died after winning an athletics race, this could so easily have been regarded as one of those tragic events with no apparent purpose.

However, within a week of Peter's death, a Tyneside man had been given a new lease of life thanks to a heart transplant, two young Lancashire folk who had been blind were able to see, and a Cotswolds man's health was greatly improved thanks to a kidney transplant.

All this because Peter Everett had said that if anything were ever to happen to him, the doctors could use any part of his body to help others. In this way the death of one young man gave a new lease of life and fresh hope to no fewer than four different people.

SATURDAY—APRIL 3.

*SUDDENLY the world is radiant 'neath a
sky of blue,*
*People smiling secretly as if dreams all come
true,*
*Green country hedgerows blossom forth in lacey
pink and white,*
*Awakening every heart to gladness, breathing
new delight.*

*Yes, suddenly it's Spring again, earth holds its
breath with joy,*
*In every heart there's magic that nothing can
destroy;*
*The ghost of Winter hides his face and quietly
slips away*
*Trailing his cloak of sadness in the shades of
yesterday.*

SUNDAY—APRIL 4.

THE fool hath said in his heart, there is no God.

MONDAY—APRIL 5.

A CERTAIN minister appeared before his
congregation one Sunday with his finger
bandaged. After the service one of the worshippers
asked a friend what had happened to the preacher's
finger.

" Oh, he told me he had his mind on his sermon
while he was shaving, and accidentally cut his
finger."

" That's too bad," said his friend. " But next
Sunday I hope he'll have his mind on his finger and
cut his sermon."

THE FRIENDSHIP BOOK

ONE often finds that the really great people in life are extraordinarily humble and have the ability to put others, less gifted than themselves, completely at ease.

John McCormack, the famous Irish tenor, had arrived in New York where he was due to sing at an important concert. That morning quite by chance he heard that an old Scots lady, now living in the States, was disappointed that because of illness she would be unable to attend the performance. John asked for her address and within a couple of hours was standing at her bedside.

" What would you like me to sing?" he asked.

The frail little lady whispered that " Bonnie Mary o' Argyll " always brought back memories of her girlhood spent in the West Highlands. Immediately John's golden voice filled the house. Then, for good measure, he recited two poems by Robert Burns.

The old lady was overjoyed and later begged the renowned singer to accept a picture of the Isle of Iona as a memento of this happy meeting. John McCormack treasured that simple picture all the days of his life. A great man, indeed.

DID you hear about the father whose birthday was in the offing? His little daughter, aged seven, asked him what he would like as a present. Dad said he didn't want anything in particular.

His little girl would not be put off. " Come on, Daddy, tell me what you want," she said. " Then give me the money and I'll go and get it for you!"

THURSDAY—APRIL 8.

I ONCE saw an old key that bore the inscription: " If I rest, I rust." I have never forgotten it. A key that is constantly being used always keeps bright and shiny, and it's not so different with people, is it? We may have limitations imposed on us by age or infirmity, but how important it is to keep as active as we can.

FRIDAY—APRIL 9.

S PRING . . . who doesn't love this season of the year? Many poets and writers have said beautiful and wise words about it, and from the great treasure of literature I pick today this single great thought from Martin Luther:

" Our Lord has written the promise of the Resurrection not in books alone, but in every leaf in springtime."

SATURDAY—APRIL 10.

W HEN April showers come along, either the real ones or those little " showers " that seem to spoil life, I always recall a little poem which I learnt as a child. I didn't enjoy learning it at the time and I don't know who wrote it, but I am often grateful for it now. Here it is:

God sends the sunshine and the rain
To make us think along the way
That life with all its ups and downs
Is like a changing April day.
It's easy to be happy through
All the sunny hours,
But we must learn to smile and sing
When sunshine turns to showers.

SUNDAY—APRIL 11.

JESUS came and spake unto them, saying, All power is given unto me in heaven and in earth.

MONDAY—APRIL 12.

SURELY the most joyous service of the year is the one held on Easter morning. If there is one day of the year when all Christians should feel optimistic it's Easter Sunday. Unfortunately some people are just not made that way. A minister told me of one Easter Day. It was a beautiful morning—the sun was shining, the birds singing, flowers were peeping through the grass and the trees and hedgerows were clothed in their first delicate green.

" What a lovely Easter Day!" he called to one of his congregation as he arrived at the church. " Oh, aye," was the reply. " But I've known it to snow well after Easter Sunday some years."

But why remember the snow when the sun is shining? In contrast, I recall the story of a woman who had been invited to attend the Harvest Thanksgiving service at a country church. She went rather reluctantly because she wasn't a great churchgoer. In any case, it had been a terrible summer—rain, rain, rain. It was still raining as she trudged to church and she couldn't help wondering to herself: " What on earth have country folk to be thankful for this year?"

Then, as she entered the church door, there in the porch was the first part of the harvest display, and right in the centre where no-one could miss it, a reminder of one of God's greatest gifts—a glass of water!

LOVELY!

No matter how busy you happen to be,
There's always just time for a nice cup of tea!

THE daughter of Karl Marx once confessed to a friend that she had never been brought up in any religion and had never been religious. " But," she said, " the other day I came across a beautiful little prayer which I very much wished could be true."

" And what prayer was that ?" asked her friend.

Slowly the daughter of Karl Marx began repeating in German the words, " Our Father, which art in heaven, hallowed be Thy Name, Thy kingdom come . . ."

EVERY 14th of April the Japanese officially remember Bill Adams. Adams was the first Englishman to enter Japan, and he did so as the chief pilot of a Dutch vessel which ran aground on the coast of Kyushu in April 1600.

He was befriended by Tokugawa Ieyasu, the Country's ruler, who persuaded Adams to stay in Japan and teach him mathematics, navigation, how Europeans lived, how they traded, and especially how they built ships. In return Adams became the ruler's diplomatic agent, was granted an estate, and married a Japanese wife.

In Tokyo today you will find an Anjin-Cho, or Pilot Street, named after Bill Adams from Chatham, who died on April 14th, 1620, having lived " in such favour with two emperors as never was any Christian in those parts of the world."

The 300th anniversary of his death was commemorated in Tokyo by the erection of a shrine on the site of the house in which he had lived.

EASTER-TIDE is always an attractive season. The cold dark days of winter have disappeared, the sun is shining, the spring flowers push their way through the brown earth. Everything betokens life and movement. And, of course, for all Christians, the commemoration of Christ's death and Resurrection means hope, joy, and peace.

William Sangster, the celebrated Methodist minister, loved Easter more than any other Christian festival. He used to say that it combines both the human and the divine in a wonderful manner. Towards the end of his life Sangster became paralysed and completely speechless. He knew that his preaching days were ended. One Easter Sunday he indicated to his family that he wanted to write. They brought him pen and paper. Then slowly, painfully, he wrote: " It is sad that no longer can I exclaim ' Alleluia! Christ is Risen!' but sadder still that there are many today who can utter those words but simply won't. They have forgotten Christ and the real meaning of Easter."

Religious faith is indeed a precious gift. As William Sangster realised, it sustains one in bitter misfortune, it offers a glimpse of the eternal and it gives a purpose to daily living.

AS the Lady of the House would tell you, I am never at my best first thing in the morning. Not that I don't try—I do, believe me. And among the words that help me are these by Elbert Hubbard: " Be pleasant till ten in the morning, and the rest of the day will take care of itself."

THE FRIENDSHIP BOOK

KATIE BEAVERS of Grantham is obviously a happy little girl. She enjoys most of the things that girls enjoy—swimming, reading and riding a pony. No one would guess that she suffers from spina bifida, for Katie bravely minimises her handicap.

Some time ago when the BBC series " Songs of Praise " visited Grantham, one of the requested items came from Katie, then aged ten. Her request? That lovely little hymn, " Glad that I live am I . . . That the sky is blue; Glad for the country lanes, And the fall of dew . . ."

LO, I am with you alway, even unto the end of the world.

HARRY was a young college graduate who worked at a textile finishing plant. Wherever his name was mentioned in the factory, it was enough to light up many faces for everybody who came into contact with him experienced the same uplift. He was living proof that life is not only worth living—it can be exciting and thrilling, too.

His mother was an invalid, and he was her major support, yet he was as cheerful and as happy with her as he was at his work. She remarked that if it hadn't been for Harry's zest for living, his exuberant attitude towards work and people, towards adversity as well as joy, she would have given up the fight for life long ago.

God bless the Harrys of this world!

TUESDAY—APRIL 20.

WHEN the Rev. Dr Hanson gave a lecture on the subject of " Fools ", his chairman was Dr. Henry Vincent, a personal friend who was also something of a humorist.

Dr. Vincent introduced him as follows: " We are now to have a lecture on fools by one "—long pause and loud laughter—" of the wisest men in the country."

The lecturer responded as follows: " I am not half so big a fool as Dr. Vincent "—long pause and loud laughter—" would have you suppose."

Playing with words and pauses, of course—but an amusing reminder that we would do well not to jump to hasty conclusions.

WEDNESDAY—APRIL 21.

I LIKED this comment from Bert Brandreth, pastor of the Methodist Church in Malvern, Pennsylvania.

There are three kinds of givers—the flint, the sponge and the honeycomb. To get anything from a flint, you must hammer it, and then you get only chips and sparks; to get water out of a sponge, you must squeeze it, and the more you squeeze the more you get; but the honeycomb just overflows with its own sweetness.

Some people are stingy and hard as flint—they give nothing away if they can help it. Others are good-natured—they yield to pressure, and the more they are pressed, the more they give. Best of all though, there are others who delight in giving without being asked. Now you know why I would rather be like a honeycomb than a flint or a sponge!

PROMISE

When days are dark and clouded—
No sunshine breaking through,
The gentians' bells remind us still
The sky above is blue.

E

THE FRIENDSHIP BOOK

I SUPPOSE one of the best-loved poems in our language is Wordsworth's daffodils. You remember how it goes:

> *Beside the lake, beneath the trees,*
> *Fluttering and dancing in the breeze.*

These lines flashed into my mind as, in the company of a friend, I strolled round the grounds of The Hirsel, the estate and family home of Sir Alec Douglas Home in the Scottish Borders.

Many of the uncountable multitude of daffodils we were seeing were the gift of the people of Holland to the great statesman on his 70th birthday. And Sir Alec, the most generous of men, is happy to share his gift with others—the grounds of The Hirsel are open to all who love peace and beauty.

I think Wordsworth would be surprised and delighted to see how many daffodils are blooming in our countryside today. Bulbs that have been cleared out of gardens, seeds that have been carried by the wind and birds; and blooms established by the kindly deeds of people like a man I know, who, whenever he has a bulb to spare, plants a little clump by the roadside.

> *THE road of life's a winding one*
> *That twists and turns its way*
> *Through joy and jubilation,*
> *Disappointment and dismay.*
> *Look yonder! Though the road may seem*
> *Uncertain, if we tread*
> *With hope and courage in our hearts,*
> *A new dawn lies ahead.*

THE FRIENDSHIP BOOK

I CAME across two quotations recently which complement each other nicely. They both concern the tendency we all have to tell everybody all about it whenever we do something for somebody else, or perhaps even just do our duty.

The first quotation is from Mark Twain: " When some men discharge an obligation you hear the report for miles around!"

The second is from Charles Lamb: " The greatest pleasure I know is to do a good action by stealth, and to have it found out by accident."

Then there is the old English saying: " Virtue is its own reward." Five words that say it all.

A ND let us not be weary in well doing: for in due season we shall reap, if we faint not.

W HEN British explorer Wilfred Thesiger visited the island village of Abu Shaja in Iraq, he stayed overnight with the local headman, who treated him with great courtesy.

However, next morning, after breakfast, the headman and his son watched Thesiger struggle with his luggage down to the canoe, and made no attempt to help. Later, Thesiger told a friend about the incident and the friend explained that in Iraq a host should always help guests to carry their things *into* the house, but not *out* of it. To do that would look as if he were in a hurry to get rid of them.

Do we sometimes appear more anxious to speed visitors on their way than to welcome them?

THANK YOU

*Blessed are they who work all day
To make a garden brave and gay.*

TUESDAY—APRIL 27.

I AM sure most of us find comfort in slipping into a small country church and sitting quietly for a few minutes. Few people leave without contributing a small " Thank you " for the upkeep of the building.

In one little church I visited, someone had left this humorous message for visitors:

If thou has aught to give or lend,
This ancient parish church befriend.
If poor, but still in spirit willing,
Out with thy purse and spare a shilling.
But if its depth should be profound
Think of thy God and give a pound.
Look not for record to be given
But trust for thy receipt in Heaven.

WEDNESDAY—APRIL 28.

MR PENDEREL, a character in J. B. Priestley's novel, *Benighted,* says rather wistfully, " We ought to go back to hour-glasses and sundials, things which deal with time quietly and don't forever pester us with their sixty seconds to a minute."

Taken literally, of course, that is hardly practicable in this highly organised world where there are buses and trains to catch, appointments to keep, schedules to fulfil. Yet " the tyranny of time " can be very real. We are sometimes so obsessed with " saving time " that we scarcely ever consider what we do—or ought to do—with the time we save.

Time is not so much to be saved as to be savoured. As Fulton Sheen once wrote, " Every moment gives us more treasures than we can gather."

THURSDAY—APRIL 29.

WHEN April chooses to smile, it is like no other month.

It is youth, hope, promise. Couples walking hand in hand in the park. Children once again discovering the magic of street games. Neighbours chatting over fences. It is the smell of freshly-turned earth, daffodils nodding sleepily in the breeze, the bright green of first leaves, shining rakes, hoes, spades and lawnmowers on the pavement in front of ironmongers' shops. April is rain at the week-ends, mud on the kitchen floor, earth stains on the knees of old jeans.

When April smiles, there is a great stirring in all the land. It is the open door.

FRIDAY—APRIL 30.

IT sounds almost too ridiculous but we have Mr Hubert Brinton's assurance that he copied down in his notebook the following conversation between a verger who was conducting a party round a famous and busy abbey and a member of the group who knelt down and prayed:

Verger: " Come along, sir!"

Visitor: " But mayn't I have a few moments of private devotion?"

Verger: " No, we can't 'ave that, or we should soon 'ave people prayin' all over the place."

I can't help feeling that the world might be a better place if, not only in churches but in homes, and schools, and offices, and workshops, and factories, and universities, and council chambers, and courts of law, and markets and anywhere else you can think of, we had a few more people " prayin' all over the place."

MAY

SOME years ago, a photographer in Munich was depressed by the impersonal appearance of huge blocks of flats in which nobody seemed to know anybody else. Then he had an idea. He would take a photograph of each of the tenants so that they could hang them in their windows facing outwards!

Nearly everyone agreed and so, in a few days practically every window in the block had a picture of its tenant looking out. Almost at once the whole atmosphere of the flats changed. People started talking to one another, calling on one another. For the first time they had become aware of one another as people, not just as flat numbers.

One of the insidious temptations of those of us who belong to the great mass of what we call "ordinary" folk is that of thinking we don't count for much. Abraham Lincoln once said, "God must have had an especial fondness for ordinary people because He made so many of them." But even ordinary people are unique. There are no two of us alike.

What we need is a bit of imagination and a bit of faith in ourselves and in human nature. Then we begin to realise that we do count, that we are not just "flat numbers" or cogs in some great impersonal machine.

FOR by grace are ye saved through faith; and that not of yourselves: it is the gift of God.

DREAMING

It's fine to let your mind run free
By little bays that meet the sea,
And wonder what the tides will bring,
What brave new tune the surges sing.
Oh, far can fancy's footsteps roam
Yet never leave the shores of home!

THE FRIENDSHIP BOOK

THIS verse has no title—it doesn't need one:
> *One step won't get you very far—you've got to*
> *keep on walking.*
> *One word won't tell folks who you are—you've*
> *got to keep on talking.*
> *One foot won't make you very tall—you've got*
> *to keep on growing.*
> *One trip to church won't tell you all—you've got*
> *to keep on going.*

PARIS in the Spring!" We have all heard about it, even if we have not seen it—the gentle warmth, the trees on the boulevards touched with a tracery of pale green, the flower-sellers with their baskets on the pavements.

On just such a morning the scene was marred by an angry gendarme accusing a middle-aged woman driver of blowing her horn in restricted hours. Almost in tears she protested her innocence, and while the argument was in process a man in the car behind got out and came to the policeman saying, " Madame is telling the truth. She did not sound her horn. It was me."

The gendarme looked from one to the other and then, without a word, he walked to the pavement, bought a bunch of violets and returning to the lady's car presented them to her with a courtly bow!

He might just have apologised graciously, and no doubt that would have been enough. But he went " the extra mile."

A simple act of courtesy can sometimes speak louder than words.

THAT great Scot, Robert Louis Stevenson, was almost as famous for his life-long courage against persistent ill-health as for the stories he wrote.

One morning when he was wracked with pain, his wife observed, " I expect you will tell me this is a glorious day."

Between bouts of coughing the author nodded and murmured, " It is. Look at the sun streaming through the window."

Then seeing her astonishment he added, " I refuse to let a row of medicine bottles be the circumference of my horizon."

WHEN Queen Mary celebrated her 80th birthday in May 1947, the BBC asked her what radio programme she would like as a special treat. She requested " something by Agatha Christie ", an author of whom she was very fond.

So the BBC broadcast a twenty-minute one-act playlet entitled *Three Blind Mice*, especially for Her Majesty's personal pleasure.

Later, Agatha Christie revised and extended Queen Mary's birthday play to a full-length production which opened in November 1952 at the Ambassadors Theatre in London's West End and has been running ever since!

It is *The Mousetrap*, which has even outlived its author, as well as making theatrical history by becoming the longest-running show in the world and bringing pleasure to many thousands of people.

THE FRIENDSHIP BOOK

A BAPTIST friend in Yorkshire sent me this excerpt from his local church magazine. Read it carefully—it's well worth it!

" Xvxn though my typxwritxr is an old modxl, It works wxll xnough xxcxpt for onx of thx kxys. I havx wishxd many timxs that it workxd pxrfxctly. It is trux thxrx arx forty-fivx kxys that function wxll xnough, but just onx kxy not working makxs all thx diffxrxncx.

So, nxxt timx you think you arx only onx pxrson and that your xffort is not nxxdxd, rxmxmbxr my typxwritxr, and say to yoursxlf, ' I am a kxy pxrson. Thx Lord nxxds mx.' "

Yes, indeed, we do all count.

E VERY spring I never fail to cheer myself up by sowing a few seeds. I buy a packet of Virginia Stock, which I'm convinced are the easiest of all seeds to grow. They will flourish in any sort of soil, in any odd corner of the garden.

I sprinkle these very dull-looking tiny brown seeds on the earth, then more or less forget about them. Yet they never fail to produce their crop of delicate little flowers in pastel shades, all sweetly scented. It's just a simple thing, which I have known ever since childhood—but there's nothing like sowing seeds for making you appreciate the wonders of this world.

B E of good courage, and he shall strengthen your heart, all ye that hope in the Lord.

THE FRIENDSHIP BOOK

ARE you troubled with insomnia? Lying awake at night is far more common than you might think, and there are all kinds of ways of tackling the problem, quite apart from asking the doctor to prescribe something. One answer is to make full use of the time you are awake. Like Blaise Pascal, the great French thinker of the 17th century. Kept awake one night with a very severe pain he started work on a notoriously difficult problem in mathematics which had baffled the best minds of his day. And he solved it! If he had tackled the problem during his waking hours he might not have seen the solution at all.

It's just another illustration of how sensible it is to fill every part of our life—even sleepless nights—by doing something useful.

CHARLES LAMB, the great English essayist, once wrote a line which I have always found true to my own experience. I thought of it the other day when we received a surprise visit from a friend. There was a hesitant tap-tap on the half-open door. We turned our heads in expectancy, and there was our friend whom we had not seen for many months.

This is what Charles Lamb wrote:

" Not many sounds exceed in interest a knock at the door."

He penned these words more than 150 years ago, but allowing for the fact that it is more likely to be a ring on a doorbell, his observation is as true as ever. May you have a knock or a ring at the door today—and may it herald a welcome guest.

GIVING THANKS

Patchwork fields and winding lanes,
Farms below the hill;
Thank God that if we search them out
There are such places still!

WEDNESDAY—MAY 12.

CAN you spare a moment?
Have you time to care?
Comfort for one who's lonely,
Someone's sorrow share?
Friendly thoughts are priceless
In this world today,
Spread a little kindness
As you pass this way.

THURSDAY—MAY 13.

DR. WILLIARD L. SPERRY tells of an American student he knew who was planning a cycle tour of England. Dr Sperry found him poring over maps, working out a route which would enable him to keep to fairly level roads and avoid the hills.

But what a way to see England! He would miss Devon and Cornwall, the Lake District, the downs and moors, and much more beside. And if he extended his tour to Scotland and Wales he would see very little indeed.

How much we miss in life if we are always seeking to " avoid the hills ", to take the easy way.

FRIDAY—MAY 14.

I HEAR often from John Campbell of Belmont, California. Every so often, one of his letters arrives on my desk with points to ponder, or simply a tongue-in-cheek comment on everyday life. Like this one recently. I'm sure it'll make you smile. Though there's a fair bit of truth in it, too:

The accent today may be mainly on youth, but most of the stress is on parents!

PETER MARSHALL, the famous American preacher, was born in Coatbridge in Lanarkshire. In his younger days, he was a keen climber and hill-walker and was often up in the hills at weekends.

One day, when the mist came down, he kept going for a while and then sat down to wait for it to clear. When at last it lifted he was stunned to find he had stopped just short of the edge of a sheer drop.

The experience had a profound effect on Marshall. He looked on it as a sign that God had spared his life because He had something worth while for him to do, and from then on he committed his life to God's work.

SUNDAY—MAY 16.

GIVE unto the Lord the glory due unto his name: worship the Lord in the beauty of holiness.

MONDAY—MAY 17.

IN the churchyard of the Derbyshire village of Hartington is the grave of a man called William Derbyshire, who departed this life in 1807. The epitaph on his gravestone speaks volumes for his character:

The man that lies beneath this stone
Was for his honesty well known;
An industrious wife he had, and children kind
Which gave satisfaction to his mind.
His debts he paid—his grave you see—
Prepare yourself to follow he!

NO HURRY

It's good to linger, stop for a chat;
There should always, ALWAYS, be time for that.

THE FRIENDSHIP BOOK

AFTER a Portsmouth businessman had interviewed an eighteen-year-old youth who had applied to him for a job, he wrote to his previous employer for a reference. The reply, which came by return of post, gave him food for thought:
" Dear Sir,

Tom was in my employ for two weeks. Any employer who gets Tom to work for him will be very lucky."

I LOOKED in to see an old friend at a limb-fitting centre. He had lost a foot as the result of an accident and I was amazed to see how well he was getting around with his new limb. The Sister was passing through the ward and she stopped to have a word with him.

" Isn't he getting on well!" I said to her.

" I knew he would," said Sister. " We can give people limbs but only the wearers can make them work."

Being a busy woman she left us. My friend touched my arm.

" Look," he said quietly. " See this little woman with the zimmer."

She was pushing the zimmer very, very slowly, puffing and panting. With a gasp and a grin she stopped beside us.

" Gosh, I'll never catch the bus at this rate," she panted.

I was wondering what to say but I needn't have worried, for with a twinkle in her eye she added, " But I'll get the next one!"

I could see what Sister had meant.

THE FRIENDSHIP BOOK

KOMUTI was a Japanese farmer whose principal product was rice. Every year when he gathered in his harvest, he piled it into great stacks ready for threshing.

One year during Harvest Festival time, Komuti was at home when he felt the earth tremble—it was the dreaded earthquake which wrecked Yokohama in 1923. From where he lived, many miles from the city, Komuti could see great waves gathering out at sea and knew that the waters would come rushing inshore soon.

How could he warn his fellow-villagers near the sea of their peril? Then he had an idea, snatched a flaming branch from his household fire and ran into his fields. He set fire to the first of his rice stacks, then the next, and before long all his rice stacks were blazing away. People down near the seashore saw the flames and clouds of smoke, and began to hurry away to fight the fire.

Soon the beaches were deserted, and when the huge waves rolled on to the seashore, there was no one there. Not a life was lost in that village, thanks to Komuti, who had sacrificed his own precious rice harvest in order to save the others' lives.

THE author and journalist Gordon Irving, who in the course of a lifelong study of show-business has visited just about every live theatre in Britain, once came out with this acute little observation which I think is well worth remembering: "Kindness is the ability to love people more than they deserve."

Think about it.

SATURDAY—MAY 22.

A LITTLE boy told his mum that he didn't want to go to Sunday School because they were going to be learning about Heaven. When Mum asked him why he didn't want to hear about it, he said, " Cos I want Heaven to be a surprise."

SUNDAY—MAY 23.

B LESSED be the Lord, because he hath heard the voice of my supplications.

MONDAY—MAY 24.

O N the high pinnacles of Lincoln Cathedral's west front stand two statues. One is of the saintly Bishop Hugh of Lincoln, and the other depicts the Swineherd of Stow. Who was he? We do not even know his name, but it is said he was tending his herd of swine when the Cathedral was being built, and as he watched, he longed to be able to contribute towards it. He scrimped and saved, often going without a meal so that he could put a coin aside, and when he had enough coins to fill his horn, he carried it to the Bishop and poured the coins at his feet.

Bishop Hugh remembered our Lord's story of the widow and her apparently small contribution—and knew that as far as God was concerned, the Swineherd of Stow had given more than all the rich people who had given out of their wealth. That is why, more than 700 years after, Bishop and Swineherd look down from Lincoln Cathedral, reminding all who pass that the Church is a living partnership of all sorts and conditions of men.

LOOK!

Though it may seem that Winter's here to stay,
Be sure that Springtime follows close behind,
Touching the garden trees with pink and white,
Scattering beauty just for us to find.

TUESDAY—MAY 25.

A WIDOW in Durham wrote to tell me of her struggle to bring up two sons after her husband died.

She isn't sorry for herself, but she does say how much she misses her husband when the boys are in bed and she has no one to talk to about the little happenings of their life. No one to give her another grown-up view to balance her own on how she's handling the boys, their hopes and school-work. Or even just to ask, " Well, what kind of day have you had?"

By the same post came another letter, from Mrs Strang, of Camelon, enclosing a verse which had been handed to her sister in America when her husband died.

I do not know who wrote it, but I pass it on, in the hope it might bring some comfort to others like the brave soul in Durham:

God hath not promised skies always blue,
Flower-strewn pathways all our lives through,
God hath not promised sun without rain,
Joy without sorrow, peace without pain.
But God hath promised strength for the day,
Rest for the labour, light for the way,
Grace for the trials, help from above,
Unfailing sympathy, undying love.

WEDNESDAY—MAY 26.

THE writer George Eliot once commented: " Not a leaf has ever fluttered down into the dust and perished there, but has helped to enrich the earth's soil; and not a lowly life in all the past has been lived purely and holy, but the world today is a little richer and better for it."

THE FRIENDSHIP BOOK

ALBERT was a very shy boy. He didn't make friends easily, much preferring his own company. His record at school was not encouraging and when his father asked his son's schoolmaster what sort of a career Albert should aim for, he was told: " It doesn't matter—he will never amount to much."

Yet when he died in 1955, Albert was acknowledged as perhaps the greatest scientist who ever lived. He had won the Nobel Prize for physics in 1921 and evolved the theory of relativity. His name was Albert Einstein.

The brilliant scientist was also the kindliest and most human of men. Perhaps because as a boy he had been so shy himself he took a great interest in young folk and loved to encourage them.

He amounted to quite a lot.

I HAVE an old friend who is a retired Durham miner and uses the local dialect known as " Pitmatic." He is now in his mid-eighties and says that he's just " scrubbin an gannin." Which means that, with some effort, he still manages to get along life's road. Recently he confessed to me that he was a little worried about the day when " me scrubbin winnit make us gan." In other words, when he prepares to meet his Maker. And he added, " Ah hope we get on all reet, etornity's a lang time."

I'm sure you can put that into your own sort of language, and when you do you'll realise what a wonderfully personal view of God my old friend has. With his simple, strongly-held faith, I don't think he has anything to worry about, do you?

THE FRIENDSHIP BOOK

TENZING NORGAY who, on the morning of 29th May, 1953, stood with Edmund Hillary on the summit of Everest, told his life story to James Ramsay Ullman who wrote it up in his book, *Man of Everest.*

Tenzing tells of how from boyhood he was fascinated by the mountains and the legends of the evil spirits that guarded the heights and would bring doom to any man who ventured there. " But," says Tenzing, " . . . I wanted to see for myself, to find out for myself. This was the dream I have had as long as I can remember. There they stood above me, the great mountains—Makalu, Lhotse, Nuptse . . . a hundred others. And towering above them all, Chomolungma—Everest. ' No bird can fly over it,' said the story. But what could a man do? A man with a dream?"

Where would the world be without its dreamers? Where should *we* be without *our* dreams?

HEAR, O Lord, when I cry with my voice: have mercy also upon me, and answer me.

OLD Granny Smith always starts to sing " Nearer, my God, to Thee ", as she cooks the breakfast.

" Is that your favourite hymn?" she was asked.

" Not really," she smiled. " But I always know that when I reach the end of the third verse, the eggs are soft-boiled!"

JUNE

TUESDAY—JUNE 1.

A WEALTHY American was admiring the lawns of an Oxford College he was visiting.

" Say," he said to the gardener, " I'd sure like a lawn like this back home. How do I begin ? "

" Well," said the old gardener slowly, " You'd need some of our good English soil."

" Oh, that's easy enough," said the American. " We can easily have a few hundred tons shipped over."

" And grass seed," said the gardener.

" That's okay too," was the reply.

" Then you've to be sure the ground's dead level before you sow in the Autumn, and the grass cut and rolled in the Spring. And cut and rolled, and cut and rolled."

" Fine," said the American. " And how long does this cutting and rolling go on ? "

" Well," said the gardener thoughtfully. " If you want a lawn like this one, I should say about a couple of hundred years."

There are no short cuts to anything worthwhile.

WEDNESDAY—JUNE 2.

THE minister was giving a lesson to a Sunday School class.

" Now, boys," he said, " suppose I saw a man beating a donkey, and stopped him, what virtue would my action show ? "

To which one bright boy replied: " Brotherly love, sir ? "

THE FRIENDSHIP BOOK

WHO is there of us who does not know Thomas
Gray's poem which begins,
The curfew tolls the knell of parting day,
The lowing herd winds slowly o'er the lea ?
When Gray first wrote that poem, we are told
that he did not like it. Nor did he like the second or
the third attempt. Indeed, if you visit the British
Museum you will be able to see the 75 drafts which
Gray made of the poem before he was satisfied!

It's worth reminding ourselves that great
achievements rarely come easily. If we are sometimes discouraged with our efforts it may help a
little to remember Thomas Gray's 75 attempts at
his " Elegy Written In A Country Churchyard."

A TRAVELLER in Papua, describing his
experiences, told how his guides and carriers
would sometimes sit down at the road-side and
refuse to go any farther without a rest. It was not
simply their bodies which were tired, they
explained. " We must give our souls a chance to
catch up with our bodies."

Tiredness is not just a physical thing. A man
may feel weary at the thought of cutting the grass,
as Dr. Leslie Weatherhead once said, yet go off
cheerfully for a strenuous round of golf!

Prayer and meditation, mental relaxation, the
stimulus of some consuming interest, the delight of
doing something to help someone else—these may
seem rather different things, but they all have this
in common: they can revive our energy, banish our
tiredness and " give our souls a chance to catch up
with our bodies."

SATURDAY—JUNE 5.

SIR BILLY BUTLIN will be remembered with gratitude by many people, not least those who have enjoyed a holiday at one of the several camps he started at half a dozen coastal resorts in Britain. Sir Billy was always cheerful, ever a showman, and a lover of his fellow-men.

He was exceedingly generous. Over the years he gave over a million pounds to different charities. He wanted his campers to have the best of everything, and to be able to enjoy a holiday at a reasonable cost, without being tied to rigid timetables.

One charitable enterprise which may not be as widely known was the free week's holiday he gave to thousands of poorly-paid clergymen.

Thank you, Sir Billy, for all the pleasure and encouragement you brought to so many.

SUNDAY—JUNE 6.

FOR we walk by faith, not by sight.

MONDAY—JUNE 7.

I READ once of a psychiatrist who asked 3000 people, " What have you to live for?" He was surprised to discover from their answers that most of them were living for the future. They were waiting for " something " to happen—waiting for their holidays, waiting for their children to grow up, waiting hopefully for promotion, waiting for retirement or much else.

Of course it's good to look to the future, but not if it means neglecting today. There is so much to be enjoyed *now*—let's make the most of it.

I THINK one of the best definitions I have ever come across is " Service is love in overalls." It is rather interesting that J. B. Phillips translates some words of Peter, " Be clothed with humility," as " Wear the overall of humility in serving each other."

All this reminds us that love is not just some starry-eyed quality but the practical, down-to-earth business of doing what we can to help one another.

Henry Ward Beecher once said, " Religion means work; it means hard work; it means work in a dirty world. The world has to be cleaned by somebody and you are not really called of God unless you are prepared to scour and scrub."

Put on your overalls!

WEDNESDAY—JUNE 9.

ON our summer holiday last year I was able to spend some time watching a river in all its moods.

On fine days the surface of the water would be calm and smooth, like beautiful, blue glass. But on windy and wet days the surface was dull grey, seething and bubbling as if it could hardly contain its anger.

Both pictures of the river were true pictures. Just like life, really. Sometimes our surfaces are smooth and sparkling in the sunlight; at other times we feel ruffled and buffeted by storm. The thing to remember is that clouds *do* pass on by, and greyness *does* turn to blue. It's just a matter of keeping afloat, waiting for the sun to break through again. It always does, you know.

THURSDAY—JUNE 10.

WILL JOHNS is a forthright man who has never been afraid to speak his mind. It came as no surprise when he was invited to become Mayor of Bath in 1974. He was considered a worthy choice.

He had no particular church allegiance, and so the question of appointing a Mayoral Chaplain required careful thought.

Then he remembered that many years before when he lay seriously wounded in a military hospital overseas, he had been visited frequently by a young woman Salvation Army Captain. When he had eventually returned to England, an equally bright and sparkling Captain had met him at the quayside.

That settled it—he was certain that the young Captain from the local Salvation Army Goodwill Centre would make an admirable chaplain.

So Irish-born Captain Molly McCormick became the first woman chaplain and, at the age of 30, the youngest-ever Chaplain of Bath.

FRIDAY—JUNE 11.

WHEN the Rev. Alan MacLeod retired in 1979 after 24 years as Principal of Westminster College, Cambridge, he attended the United Reformed Church Annual Assembly and spoke of how he disliked votes of thanks which sacrifice honesty to kindness.

A few minutes later he chuckled heartily as he approved the painstaking honesty of the Church Life report which read: " The retirement of Principal Alan MacLeod is recorded with great gratitude "!

BEST OF ALL

Of course it's good to travel,
See the world the sailor's way,
But the greatest thrill is knowing,
" I am going home today!"

THE FRIENDSHIP BOOK

THOMAS EDISON never stopped searching for new and better ways to do things. Once, while working on his storage battery, he made eight thousand tests without success. An assistant asked if he wasn't discouraged.

" Why should I feel downhearted?" replied Edison. " We've made a lot of progress. At least we know 8,000 things that *won't* work!"

The remark was typical of Edison's attitude towards science. He believed in practical experiments rather than in theories. It was he who defined genius as " 1 per cent inspiration and 99 per cent perspiration ", and declared that " there is no substitute for hard work."

HE that loveth not his brother whom he hath seen, how can he love God whom he hath not seen?

IDA RUSSELL is a lovely lass. I was delighted when her engagement was announced to Jack Grant, the popular captain of the local cricket team.

Jack's family was a large one, and they all took Ida to their hearts. The thing that pleased Ida most was what her future father-in-law said to her on the eve of the wedding: " If I were Jack, I would choose you, too!"

Fatherly words of genuine affection which could only encourage a good relationship between a new bride and her in-laws.

THE FRIENDSHIP BOOK

WHEN the author G. K. Chesterton died there was found in one of his earliest notebooks this little homily which summed up the gratitude for life that had inspired him to great things:

Here dies another day
During which I have had eyes, ears, hands
And the great world around me;
And with tomorrow begins another.
Why am I allowed two?

I CAN never walk round my garden in June with its masses of multi-coloured Russell lupins without thinking of the remarkable story of the humble jobbing gardener who created them.

George Russell went to work as a gardener's boy at the age of ten, working long hours in all weathers. It was not until he was over fifty that he found time to work seriously on his experiments, crossing and recrossing his lupins to produce from the original straggling blue flowers the straight, rounded colourful specimens which eventually brought him fame across the world.

He could have made a fortune from the plants which he refused to sell to the experts, but would simply say, " These flowers are my children. How can I sell them?"

Many honours came to him in the horticultural world, but as one of his biographers has said, " His greatest reward was in knowing that he had brought a little more beauty into the world."

We may not be able to do it exactly in George Russell's way, but is there any finer thing we can do than bring a little more beauty into the world?

THE FRIENDSHIP BOOK

IT was high summer and the Lady of the House and I thought we'd make the most of the sunshine, so we spent the day walking in the country. At tea-time, as we looked for a suitable place to unpack our picnic, my wife said, " Let's find a tree. We can use it as a canopy to shade us as we eat, and if there should be a rain-shower it'll make a fine umbrella."

We found our tree—a tall, young beech covered in new leaves—and while we enjoyed our alfresco meal we were entertained by the antics of a playful baby squirrel. Background music was free, provided by a blackbird up on the topmost branch.

It was certainly a lovely day, one I shall always remember. And now, whenever I see a tree dressed in summer-green, I think of all its many uses, and I am reminded of the words of Samuel Taylor Coleridge, who said, " Friendship is a sheltering tree."

FRIDAY—JUNE 18.

I'VE just been tidying up the garden. Most of the work—and pretty back-breaking it was, too—consisted of pulling up weeds. The problem, as I see it, is not getting the right things to grow, but preventing the wrong things from growing in their place.

Isn't it rather like that in life? If we can get rid of the little things that shouldn't be there—the bad habits, unkind remarks, and so on—the good things will grow of their own accord.

How nice if your life and mine could be like a well-tended garden.

THE FRIENDSHIP BOOK

D R LINTON-BOGLE was a family doctor who practised for more than twenty years in the Sussex village of Ditchling. When he died in 1964 the villagers got together to discuss how they could record their love and affection for him. The result is a plaque in Ditchling's High Street which reads:

In grateful affection
for the life of our Doctor
Frederick Wallace Linton-Bogle
who practised hereabouts and died 1964.

Guerir quelquefois, soulager souvent, consoler toujours.

To heal sometimes, to relieve often, to comfort always.

It is easy sometimes for us to take for granted the care and wise advice of a good doctor. The people of Ditchling have not forgotten.

S HEW me thy ways, O Lord; teach me thy paths.

PRAYER FOR A FATHER
M ENDER of toys, leader of boys,
Changer of fuses, kisser of bruises,
Bless him, dear Lord.
Mover of couches, soother of ouches,
Pounder of nails, teller of tales,
Reward him, O Lord.
Raker of leaves, cleaner of eaves,
Dryer of dishes, fulfiller of wishes,
Bless him, O Lord.

TUESDAY—JUNE 22.

IN St. Leonard's Church, Hythe, Kent, I found this " Motorist's Prayer." I think it has a message for every driver.

Give me a steady hand, a watchful eye,
That none may suffer hurt when I pass by.
Thou givest life; I pray no act of mine
May take away or mar that gift of Thine.
Shield those, dear Lord, who bear me company,
From foolish folk and all calamity.
Teach me to use my car for others' need,
Let me not miss, through witless love of speed,
The beauties of thy world. That thus I may
With joy and courtesy go on my way.

WEDNESDAY—JUNE 23.

WHEN Winston Churchill reached his 77th birthday he wrote, " We are happier in many ways when we are old than when we are young. The young sow wild oats. The old grow sage."

I am reminded, too, of the words of the late Rev. G. Bramwell Evans (who for many years was widely known as " Romany " for his nature programmes on BBC radio): " Age may wrinkle the skin, but by the grace of God it need never wrinkle the soul."

The term " growing old " is an interesting one. " Old " gives the impression of decrepitude, but " growing " suggests life and progress and development, and there *is* a growth that the passing years alone can bring us. In the familiar though anonymous words, " Youth is not a time of life; it is a state of mind." That is surely what the Psalmist meant when he said, ". . . thy youth is renewed like the eagle's."

THE FRIENDSHIP BOOK

DO we, I wonder, always appreciate the loyalty of our friends as much as we should? Mrs M. Dinmore of Norbury, London, sent me these verses in which she gives thanks for the gift of a good friend:

A friend in need is a friend indeed,
And a friend indeed have I,
Who shares my leisure, my work and pleasure,
Growing closer as time goes by.

Memories we share, both sad and gay,
And many an evening remember
Convivial talk, or a countryside walk,
In Springtime or golden September.

No words do we need, our eyes only heed
Feelings we each know are there.
Yes, Friendship is fine, and if yours is like mine,
Then God has answered a prayer.

IT'S always easy to pick faults in other people. None of us is perfect after all. The sad thing is that many people seem to find it so difficult to overlook faults in others. They ignore the good things in a person's character and concentrate on the bad.

A Persian writer once said it all:

" If you know a man who has ten faults and one good quality, try to think as little of the faults as you can, and to make the most of his one good quality. And if you know a man who has ten virtues and one fault, praise him for the former and do all you can to forget the latter."

JUST WAIT

There's much in life can be revealed
   By simply leaning over gates.
No need to travel far afield:
   The world will come to him who waits.

SATURDAY—JUNE 26.

JOHN GOUGH is not a name with which many people would be familiar. He was the son of a tradesman in Kendal, and had been blinded by smallpox when only two years old. But he was a keen student of nature, a clever scholar and mathematician, and it was he who first set the example of keeping a meteorological journal. He prompted another young man to start keeping a diary of weather conditions, and the latter readily acknowledged his indebtedness to his blind mentor when his study of the elements led him to consider the properties of gases—and later the Atomic Theory.

Had it not been for blind John Gough, Manchester might never have had John Dalton, pioneer of Atomic Theory.

SUNDAY—JUNE 27.

FOR as in Adam all die, even so in Christ shall all be made alive.

MONDAY—JUNE 28.

A FRIEND of ours called Anna has found new joy and an added measure of tranquillity —and it's all due to a simple discovery she made, which she has asked me to pass on to you.

Whereas she used to demand *more* from God in her prayers, she now says, on waking each morning, " Thank you, God, for the abundance of blessings I've already *had*. And thank you for the wonderful gift of the day ahead."

Simple, isn't it. And if it has worked for Anna, it can work for you, too.

TUESDAY—JUNE 29.

HERE'S a story from America. A Connecticut woman had a beautiful flower garden in which she took great pride. She wasn't content, however, simply to enjoy it herself. She wanted others to share its beauty so she had two large baskets fastened to the gate of the garden and every morning she filled them with masses of freshly cut flowers. In front of the baskets was a notice inviting passers-by to help themselves.

Children on their way to school, men setting out for business, women on their shopping expeditions, they all gratefully and happily responded to the invitation.

A friend said to the woman, " I know that everyone appreciates your kindness and thoughtfulness, but aren't you afraid you will rob yourself?"

" Not at all," was the reply. " I find that the more I cut, the more I seem to have."

She had stumbled on a great secret—a secret we can each learn for ourselves. Giving lovingly never makes us poor; it enriches us as nothing else can.

WEDNESDAY—JUNE 30.

GLADYS AYLWARD, the famous and much loved Englishwoman, was once asked why she became a missionary. She said that she was " absolutely, positively sure " that it was what God wanted her to do. And she gave this advice: " Whatever you do in life, say your prayers. Don't just talk to God. Be very still and quiet and give him a chance to talk to you—you'll be surprised what he has to say."

JULY

THURSDAY—JULY 1.

CHARLES HADDON SPURGEON, who lived from 1834 to 1892, was a very famous Baptist preacher, and generally agreed to have been one of the greatest orators of the 19th century. Though he became famous, and was accustomed to being the principal speaker before great audiences, Spurgeon never lost his admiration for those not so much in the public eye. One day he wrote this little verse:

It needs more skill that I can tell
To play the second fiddle well.

Our job may be quite a lowly one. We may not get any public recognition. But let us do it to the very best of our ability. Where would an orchestra be without the second fiddles?

FRIDAY—JULY 2.

LAST summer I visited the old village church at Staunton Harold in Leicestershire and read this inscription over the entrance porch:

" In the year 1653, when all things sacred throughout this realm were either demolished or profaned, Sir Robert Shirley founded this Church, whose singular praise it is to have done the best things in the worst of times, and to have hoped them in the most calamitous."

There will always be people who will put off doing something worthwhile because " it's not the right time for it." And there will always be those who—like Sir Robert Shirley—deliberately choose the darkest and most difficult hour in which to demonstrate their faith.

SATURDAY—JULY 3.

THE Reverend Ronald Jobling is now retired, but he still chuckles when he recalls the words of a worthy who shook his hand at the end of his first three year appointment at a Bolton Methodist Church.

"Well, goodbye, lad," the man said. "Tha'rt not as bad as when tha came!"

SUNDAY—JULY 4.

THE Lord is nigh unto them that are of a broken heart; and saveth such as be of a contrite spirit.

MONDAY—JULY 5.

F. AUSTIN HYDE, a headmaster of Lady Lumley Grammar School, Pickering, and a Methodist preacher, once told this true tale:

The parent of one of the boys at his school brought his son's report to him, saying, "We can't make out this comment written by one of the teachers. We all had a shot at it, in fact we made it into a party game and all wrote down what we thought it might mean. Do you mind interpreting?"

My Hyde tried and could not read it either so he said, "It's Mr Smith's writing. I'll send for him."

When Mr Smith came in Mr Hyde asked, "Do you mind interpreting this remark on Johnson's report, please?"

Mr Smith studied it for a few minutes frowning hard then said, "Oh, yes—must be more careful with his handwriting!"

TUESDAY—JULY 6.

A PARTY of American tourists were being guided through the Houses of Parliament when they suddenly met the dignified figure of the Lord Chancellor, Lord Hailsham, in full wig and gown. At that moment he spotted Neil Martin, the Conservative M.P. for Banbury.

" Neil!" called out Lord Hailsham in his usual ebullient style.

And the respectful transatlantic visitors did!

WEDNESDAY—JULY 7.

GODRIC, an old hermit, sat in the open doorway of his hut on the wooded banks of the River Wear, listening to the trees rustling and the water murmuring. Suddenly there was a crashing in the undergrowth, the thud of horses' hooves and the baying of dogs. Then a young stag appeared in the clearing, trembling with fear.

" Come!" he called gently, and the animal trotted past him into the hut. Godric closed the door and sat down again outside the hut. Suppose he was questioned, what should he say? How could he tell a lie? And yet if he told the truth . . .

For a moment he closed his eyes and prayed: " Lord, give me the words to speak."

The huntsmen appeared, and one called out to him: " Where is the stag, old man? Which way did he go?"

" God knows where he may be," said Godric gently.

" We have lost him," said the huntsman to the others, and they rode away.

" Thank you, Lord," said Godric, raising his eyes to Heaven.

H

THE FRIENDSHIP BOOK

JAMES BOSWELL was one of the best-known men of his day. He wrote the celebrated biography of Samuel Johnson, the man who compiled our first real dictionary.

Boswell loved good company. Of him Johnson said that he never visited a house without his hosts hoping for his speedy return. What a happy memory for anyone to leave behind!

DO you remember how, when Robinson Crusoe was ship-wrecked on his desert island and had salvaged all he could from the wreck of the ship, he drew up a kind of " balance sheet " of his circumstances? " I began to comfort myself as well as I could," he said, " and to set the good against the evil. And I stated it very impartially, the comforts I enjoyed against the miseries I suffered."

Here is part of his " balance sheet ": " I am cast upon a horrible desert island . . . but I am alive and not drowned . . . I have no clothes to cover me, but I am in a hot climate. I am without any defence or means to resist any violence of man or beast, but I am cast on an island where I see no wild beasts to hurt me. I have no soul to speak to or relieve me, but God wonderfully sent the ship in near enough to the shore that I have got out so many necessary things."

And then he concluded (and here, surely, is a philosophy we might well all take to heart), " Upon the whole, here was an undoubted testimony that there was scarce any condition in the world so miserable, but that there was something negative, or something positive to be thankful for in it."

SATURDAY—JULY 10.

A RABBI and a soap-maker went for a walk together. The soap-maker said, " What good is religion? Look at the trouble and misery in the world after thousands of years of religion. If religion is true, why should this be?"

The rabbi said nothing. They continued walking until he noticed a child, filthy with mud and grime, playing in the gutter. The rabbi said, " Look at that child. You say that soap makes people clean. We've had soap for generations, yet look how dirty that child is! Of what value is soap?"

The soap-maker protested, " But, Rabbi, soap can't do any good unless it is used!"

" Exactly," smiled the rabbi.

SUNDAY—JULY 11.

W AIT on the Lord: be of good courage, and he shall strengthen thine heart: wait, I say, on the Lord.

MONDAY—JULY 12.

B USH HOUSE is an office block in London with Greek-style columns, all of which have ornamental carvings except one. It was left unfinished on purpose. This is an ancient custom going back to the ancient Greeks who believed that only the work of the gods could be perfect, so they left some part unfinished as a sign of human frailty.

Of all the pillars on Bush House I think that plain one must be the most beautiful of all. It speaks, not of man's endeavour or pride, but of his humility.

A COTTAGE WINDOW

TUESDAY—JULY 13.

I SAW a short, sharp sentence the other day, written up outside a church, and it had more impact than a whole sermon on the value of prayer for those in trouble. It simply read:

" *If your knees tremble—kneel on them.* "

WEDNESDAY—JULY 14.

IN Galsworthy's famous *Forsyte Saga* Jolyon Forsyte, when a boy of eight, asked his mother, " What is beauty?"—not an easy question for anyone to answer. " Can I *see* it?" he persisted, when his mother hesitated.

" You do, every day," she replied. " The sky is beautiful, the stars and moonlight nights, and then the birds, the flowers, the trees, they're all beautiful. Look out of the window, there's beauty for you."

" Oh," said Jolyon, " that's the view. Is that all?"

Then suddenly a thought seemed to strike him. He came to his mother and put his arms round her neck and said, with all the awe of having made a wonderful discovery, " I know! You are it really, and all the rest is make-believe."

We say sometimes that " Beauty is in the eye of the beholder." What young Jolyon had discovered, of course, and what it is open to all of us to discover, is that beauty is in the eye (and the heart) of one who loves.

It is love for our work, for the people with whom we come into contact, for books, for music, for art, for the world of nature, for the everyday blessings of life that enables us to behold beauty. When we *love*, as Jolyon said, " that is it!"

THURSDAY—JULY 15.

IN 1905 it was discovered that Winchester Cathedral was sinking into a bog; walls and buttresses were leaning, great cracks were showing everywhere, and stones were falling from the high walls. The Dean and Chapter of the Cathedral called in the engineers, who discovered that the walls would not stand the vibrations of hammers, and the marshy foundations would not stand pumping dry. There was only one thing for it—and so they called in William Walker, a diver.

For more than five years Walker worked beneath the Cathedral. Section by section he grouted, cleaned, and underpinned the whole of the building. He removed the peat handful by handful, replacing it with four layers of concrete bags on the gravel bottom, followed by the pumping of water from the specific pit in which he was working. He went from pit to pit, working always in darkness, until at last he had relaid the foundations of Winchester Cathedral with his own hands, and made them secure.

Small wonder that there was great rejoicing and a special Thanksgiving Service on St Swithin's Day in 1912. The Archbishop of Canterbury preached, and William Walker, diver, sat there listening, content in the knowledge that he had saved this great shrine of English history.

If ever you visit the Cathedral you can see the memorial to him in the Lady Chapel.

FRIDAY—JULY 16.

THERE is an old Chinese proverb, " Better to light a small candle than curse the darkness." It's worth remembering.

THE FRIENDSHIP BOOK

ONE day at a time is all you may plan,
No one can tell the length of life's span;
Never fuss about trifles, it's not worth the heat,
Make the most of each hour till the day is
complete.

It's a wonderful world, look around and you'll see,
Live each moment in joy with a heart light and
free;
Past moments are dead and tomorrow unborn,
Every soul has rebirth with the first flush of dawn.

GOOD and upright is the Lord: therefore will he teach sinners in the way.

ELIZABETH ANN LINLEY was a concert singer at the age of only sixteen. She was a lovely girl, and her portrait was painted at least twice by Thomas Gainsborough. Then she fell in love. In fact there were two young men who loved her, but she had eyes for only one of them. She ran away with her schoolboy sweetheart and they were married secretly in Paris.

In later life Richard Brinsley Sheridan became even better known than his lovely wife. He wrote such plays as *The Rivals*, one of the wittiest dramas of all time, and *School for Scandal*.

But it was to his teenage sweetheart that Sheridan paid the most perfect compliment. He said to her: " Won't you come into the garden? I would like my roses to see you."

TUESDAY—JULY 20.

A PACIFIST called Bernard Pike was addressing a crowd in the open air in London. When he had finished speaking, a stranger who had been disagreeing with what Bernard had been saying, stepped up to him and punched him in the stomach. A few seconds later Bernard's attacker slumped to the ground, saying he felt unwell. Bernard at once found out where the man lived, ordered a taxi for him and paid his fare home.

Bernard the pacifist had won the fight without a single blow in retaliation!

WEDNESDAY—JULY 21.

I LIKE this anonymous little poem, called Our Choice:

Not what we have, but what we use,
Not what we see, but what we choose;
These are the things that mar or bless
The sum of human happiness.

The thing nearby, not that afar,
Not what we seem, but what we are;
These are the things that make or break,
That give the heart its joy or ache.

Not what seems fair, but what is true,
Not what we dream, but the good we do;
These are the things that shine like gems,
Like stars in fortune's diadems.

Not as we take, but as we give,
Not as we pray, but as we live;
These are the things that make for peace,
Both now and after time shall cease.

THURSDAY—JULY 22.

A LITTLE boy was fascinated by the smell and feel of newly-baked bread. He kept asking where it came from, how it was made, and so on. His mind was still full of it when an old aunt called and, patting him on the head, asked him, " What are you going to be when you grow up?"

There was no hesitation. " A loafer!" he said brightly.

FRIDAY—JULY 23.

IT is said that a surgeon, an architect and a politician were once discussing whose profession was the oldest.

" Mine is," said the surgeon. " Because a surgical operation was performed when Eve was created by the removal of a rib from Adam."

" No," said the architect. " Before that it required an architect to create an orderly universe out of chaos."

" Ah," said the politician. " But who created the chaos in the first place?"

SATURDAY—JULY 24.

ROBERT EDWARD LEE has been described as the best of the generals during the American Civil War. He hated slavery, and he hated the idea of the United States being torn apart by civil war.

He never wanted to fight against his own countrymen, and in all his correspondence and papers, it is impossible to find a single malignant word about his foes. He once wrote to his wife, " I pray for them every day."

He was a great soldier—and a great man.

SUNDAY—JULY 25.

BEAR ye one another's burdens, and so fulfil the law of Christ.

MONDAY—JULY 26.

I HEARD this story from a friend who had been watching a funeral cortège go slowly by. No one paid much attention to it—except an old tramp. He put down his bundle at his feet and removed his hat as a mark of respect. Not until the procession had gone by did he pick up his load and continue on his way.

Truly a gentleman of the road, don't you think?

TUESDAY—JULY 27.

HOW often we mar our happiness by " thinking the worst." The pianist Arthur Rubinstein, who is as loquacious in seven other languages as he is in his own, tells how he was once greatly worried by an attack of hoarseness. None of the ordinary, simple remedies seemed to help, so he made an appointment with a throat specialist.

" I searched his face for a clue during the 30-minute examination," said Rubinstein, " but it was expressionless. Then he told me to come back the next day. I went home full of fears and didn't sleep that night."

The next day there was another prolonged examination and another ominous silence on the part of the specialist.

At last Rubinstein could stand it no longer. " Tell me," he exclaimed. " I can stand the truth. I've lived a full, rich life. What's wrong with me?"

The specialist replied, " You talk too much!"

THE FRIENDSHIP BOOK

HARRY WEBB has now been in show business for well over twenty years. He has been "Top of the Pops" many times, and is popular with young and old. He is respected everywhere because he has a strength of character which endears him to many, even those who do not share his Christian ideals and beliefs.

A housewife of 30, who describes herself as a typical fan, respects his strength of purpose in living a distinctly untrendy life, whilst his music has matured over the years.

A teenager half her age comments that "whenever I hear people making fun of the life he leads, I wonder if that person has done half as much for less fortunate people as he has."

Harry Webb, better known as Cliff Richard, has not only given tremendous pleasure to many people for two full decades—he continues to support underprivileged folk throughout the world.

Thank you, Cliff!

WE have so much to be thankful for in this world, I often wonder if we realise how fortunate we are. Today I am determined to look around me and admire all the beauty that, on other days, I tend to overlook.

It was Ralph Waldo Emerson who once urged his readers with these words:

"Never lose an opportunity of seeing anything that is beautiful, for beauty is God's handwriting—a wayside sacrament. Welcome it in every fair face, in every fair sky, in every flower—and thank God for it as a cup of blessing."

GRAND DESIGN

However hard an artist tries
In capturing a scene,
Nature's canvas—simple, pure—
Will always reign supreme.

FRIDAY—JULY 30.

FIFTY years ago, George Lansbury was the leader of the Labour Party, an M.P. and a great Christian. One day he was asked for his autograph, and he thumbed through the pages of the album to see what others had written.

He found a page where someone had put: " All I want is justice."

Lansbury added underneath: " But I want love and mercy as well."

SATURDAY—JULY 31.

A YOUNG Yorkshireman stood on the top of a small hill, looked into the valley below, and dreamed. He would build the most wonderful mill in Europe down there.

Well, he did more than that. He was determined to prove to businessmen and manufacturers everywhere that they could afford to make the welfare of their workers a prime consideration. So he himself consulted his workpeople about the plans for the houses he intended to build, and built two, three, and four-bedroomed houses according to the need expressed. Some of the houses had small gardens.

By 1872 he had built 820 houses in his model village, as well as baths, schools, wash-houses and almshouses, a library and a club.

The name of the village is Saltaire, which was described then as the happiest and healthiest working community in the world, and remains as a memorial to a great dreamer—Titus Salt, the second Mayor of Bradford, an essentially shy and humble man who was regarded by his workers as their friend.

AUGUST

E VERY man according as he purposeth in his heart, so let him give; not grudgingly, or of necessity: for God loveth a cheerful giver.

O VER a hundred years ago, James Evans went to live among the North American Indians as a missionary. One summer he set off up the Hudson River in his tin canoe which the Indians had christened " The Island of Light " because it shone in the sunshine. An Indian named Hassal sat in the prow, and another Indian sat in the stern with Evans between them. They were going to visit Hassal's native tribe, the Chippewayans.

On the journey they saw some ducks, and Evans grabbed his rifle to shoot. However, a terrible accident occurred—and Evans shot Hassal dead. Although James Evans knew quite well that the fierce Chippewayans would demand his life for Hassal's, he went on to tell them what had happened.

Only one voice was not raised in anger—and that was the voice of Hassal's old mother. She had seen the love in the missionary's eyes, and pleaded with her infuriated tribe. " He didn't intend to kill," she said. " And see how bravely he has come, unarmed, and put his life in our hands. Let him live and he shall be my son in place of the one I have lost."

And to the end of his life, James Evans treated the old Indian squaw as his own mother.

THE FRIENDSHIP BOOK

IT is everlasting. Money cannot buy it. It is our most precious possession, and yet we often abuse it. From the moment we are born we seek it, but when we find it we are apt to take it for granted. The more we give it away, the more we have left.

What is it?

The answer is love.

HOLIDAYS always remind me of the story of the small boy who was howling on one of our seaside beaches—presumably because he couldn't do something, or have something, which he wanted. His mother was shaking him violently and saying, " Look! Are you going to enjoy yourself, or have I got to make you?"

But that's just the trouble—if people are determined not to enjoy themselves there is nothing we can do or say about it. Going away on holiday won't do it. A change of scenery won't do it. Happiness is not in our circumstances but in ourselves.

Looking for happiness is perhaps the surest way of missing it. It is really a kind of by-product that comes to us when we are thinking of something quite different from enjoying ourselves. The artist no doubt finds happiness in painting, but he does not say, " I am going to find happiness today." He says, " I am going to paint a picture."

We most truly enjoy ourselves when we forget ourselves and immerse ourselves in something which captures our imagination and engrosses our interest.

THERE are few things more attractive than the tall, majestic sunflower in full bloom.

According to legend, a beautiful girl fell in love with Apollo the Sun God, and longed for him to fall in love with her. But Apollo had many loves and though for a time he devoted his attention to the girl, he eventually deserted her, breaking her heart.

When they saw her sadness, the other gods took pity on the girl and turned her into a sunflower, hoping that she would forget Apollo. Even when changed to a flower the girl could not forget the Sun God; she twisted her stem so that her face could watch his journey across the sky. She still does to this day. Just look at the next sunflower you see.

FRIDAY—AUGUST 6.

GOING HOME

I'VE wandered afar through the long summer
    days
And savoured new places, and faces and things,
But now I am tired, and long for old ways,
Old friends, my own hearth, and the comfort it
    brings.

Far fields are bonnie, and far hills are high,
And new paths are pleasant to find and to roam,
But summer is over—I bid them goodbye,
There's no use denying the call to go home.

The road winds before me, I sing as I go,
And the miles slip behind me, by one and by one;
Remembering friendships, the scenes that I know,
I hasten on homeward, my wandering done.

NEVER GIVE UP!

Big or little, if fishers we be,
On one great truth we all agree—
Though today we make no score
There's always better days in store.

THE FRIENDSHIP BOOK

I LIKE this anonymous little verse entitled " Was
It You?"
Somebody did a golden deed,
Someone proved a friend in need,
Somebody sang a beautiful song,
Somebody smiled the whole day long,
Somebody thought, " 'Tis sweet to live,"
Somebody said, " I'm glad to give,"
Somebody fought a valiant fight,
Somebody lived to shield the right.
Was that somebody you?

M Y grace is sufficient for thee: for my strength
is made perfect in weakness.

H ERE are some thoughts on the theme of
friendship:

One loyal friend is worth ten thousand
relatives—Euripides.

A friend is a person with whom I may be
sincere. Before him I may think aloud—Ralph
Waldo Emerson.

Your friend is the man who knows all about
you, and still likes you—Elbert Hubbard.

We never know the true value of friends. While
they live we are too sensitive of their faults; when
we have lost them we see only their virtues—J. C.
and A. W. Hare.

Tis sweet, as year by year we lose
Friends out of sight, in faith to muse
How grows in paradise our store.—Keble.

THE FRIENDSHIP BOOK

G. K. CHESTERTON told the story of a yachtsman who saw land ahead and thought it was an unknown island inhabited by a savage race. Armed to the teeth he landed on the beach and, speaking in sign language, planted the British flag on Brighton Pavilion!

A foolish story, perhaps—yet how much more exciting life would be if we could, so to speak, " rediscover " some of the familiar things which we take so much for granted, see them as though we were seeing them for the first time. There is so much to be rediscovered about the place where we live, about the people we know, about the work we do, and indeed, about everything with which we come into contact—and most of all, perhaps, about ourselves. Let's do a bit of re-discovery!

ONE of the most thrilling lawn tennis matches at Wimbledon was the Women's Singles Final of 1978, in which Chris Evert lost to Martina Navratilova by two sets to one.

As she lost, Miss Evert ran up to her conqueror and affectionately stroked her hair.

Two years later, as Mrs. Evert-Lloyd, she reached (and lost) the Women's Singles Final again. On the way she defeated Andrea Jaeger, then only 15, but an up-and-coming star. She kept encouraging the teenager with jokes and quips as they changed over between games—and no-one minds too much losing to someone who can make them laugh.

It all goes to show that Chris Evert-Lloyd is as gracious in victory as she is generous in defeat.

MEMORY

I know each pool, each bush, each rock
Along my favourite stream,
And years away, I see them clear,
In waking or in dream.

THE FRIENDSHIP BOOK

A TOWNSMAN was sympathising with a farmer about the vagaries of the weather, and the uncertainty of gathering in the harvest successfully. " But you seem to take it all pretty calmly," he said. " I am afraid that if I were in your position I'd be worried to death about the prospects."

" No, not if you had my experience you wouldn't," said the old farmer as he pulled away at his pipe.

" Your experience ?" queried the townsman.

" Yes," replied the farmer quietly. " You see I've been farming round here for nearly fifty years, and though some years have been better than others, I've gathered in every harvest except one."

" Oh, was that when the harvest failed ?"

" Who said anything about failing ?" said the farmer. " I am talking about this year's harvest—I haven't started on it yet."

What a difference it makes to our outlook if we can look back with gratitude and look forward with hope as the old farmer clearly did.

CHILDREN do bring sunshine into our lives, don't they? When I got home the other evening little Benny from down the road was just leaving and the Lady of the House was smiling broadly. The youngster had pointed to a magazine on the table and asked, " Is that yours ?"

" Yes," she said, " But you can look through it if you want."

" Thanks," he had said, rolled it up like a telescope and put it to his eye!

THE FRIENDSHIP BOOK

YOU will find some of the richest farmland in England around Holkham in Norfolk. Yet it was not always so. In the 18th century the Holkham Hall estate was owned by Thomas Coke. One day a tenant farmer refused to renew his lease of five shillings an acre, protesting that the soil was sour and useless. Coke took on the task of working the land himself. He was so successful that it was said the estate income rose " from five to upwards of twenty thousand pounds a year."

Thomas Coke showed that hard work and diligence can work miracles—even in the poorest soil.

FOR ye know the grace of our Lord Jesus Christ, that, though he was rich, yet for your sakes he became poor, that ye through his poverty might be rich.

TED MOLE retired from the steel industry in which he had worked as an internal auditor. Wondering what to do with his retirement he volunteered for service as a missionary, and after a few weeks' training this intrepid widower went out to Sierra Leone to be business manager at Segbwema Hospital.

His attitude to his new role? " 99 per cent. God and 1 per cent. me will make something of it."

Just one example of present-day folk who heed Isaiah's age-old challenge: " Lord—here am I, send me."

THE FRIENDSHIP BOOK

CORRIE TEN BOOM, the elderly Dutch spinster who survived the horrors of the Nazi concentration camps, records that she once visited a Weavers' school where the students were making beautiful patterns. She asked them: " When you make a mistake, do you have to cut it out and start again from the beginning?"

One of the students replied: " No, our teacher is such a great artist that when we make a mistake he uses it to improve the beauty of the pattern."

Isn't that the most encouraging thing to do? Not to condemn or criticise mistakes in a negative way, but to build around them or upon them so that in the end we may profit by what is made of our mistakes.

YOU may not have heard of Michael Fenwick but he achieved a certain fame in that he was mentioned in John Wesley's *Journal*. This was something he wanted, in fact he had asked the great preacher to mention him by name. Wesley agreed to do it and the reference reads: " At noon preached to 3000 people. None seemed unmoved save Michael Fenwick who fell asleep under a haystack."

That wasn't quite the fame that Michael Fenwick had looked for! How much better if he had been content to be simply an eager listener, a quiet follower of John Wesley. " Making a name for ourselves " is much less important than living a life remembered for its honesty and helpfulness—recorded in what the Bible calls " The Book of Life."

THURSDAY—AUGUST 19.

A FIVE-YEAR-OLD, just started school, came home the other day and asked mum if he could bring a new pal to the house to play with.

Now his mum had become increasingly aware they live in a pretty mixed community. She hesitated, then, feeling rather guilty, asked, " Is he a coloured boy?"

Gordon looked puzzled for a moment, then replied, " I don't know—but I'll find out tomorrow, if you like."

Through the eyes of a child . . .

FRIDAY—AUGUST 20.

A MINISTER friend tells me of a service in the College Chapel when he was a student. The Principal was leading worship and when he came to the usual Scripture reading he announced, " I shall read from the Acts of the Apostles, chapter about ten thousand!" Then, instead of reading from the Bible he read a letter from a missionary, who was an old student of the college, telling of the work that he was doing in Africa.

This was the Principal's vivid way of reminding the students that the Acts of the Apostles was really an unfinished book, a record of work that was being continued down the ages, a work in which they, too, in their own particular way, could have a share.

That story reminded me of the remark of a man engaged not in what we would narrowly think of as " religious work," but in an ambitious scheme of irrigation which would greatly increase food production. " Isn't it wonderful," he said, " How much God has left unfinished for us to do?"

ESCAPE

Far from the busy streets of towns,
Under a different sky,
There's rest and peace and solace in
Places that Time's passed by.

THE FRIENDSHIP BOOK

TWO men behind me in a bus, one a surveyor it seemed, were discussing a house. The surveyor gave a chilling account of possible dry rot, poor ventilation and inadequate soundproofing. " I know all that," the other man said uncomfortably. " The trouble is, my wife's fallen in love with it."

But can any house be perfect? For instance, do you have a window that won't lock properly and which you hope a burglar will never discover? A spot on your lawn that eats up seed, compost and water, yet won't grow grass? A tap that starts to drip only when you're having trouble getting to sleep?

Then take comfort. You haven't got a house. You've got a home!

BUT the fruit of the Spirit is love, joy, peace, long suffering, gentleness, goodness, faith.

A SALESMAN told me this story.

A table, on order for months, had just arrived, and he phoned up his customer to let her know. A small boy answered. He sounded about three or four. " Is there anyone else I can speak to, sonny?" the salesman asked patiently, after a few minutes' unsuccessful conversation. " There's my sister," the voice at the other end piped. " Good," said the man. " Would you put her on, please?"

There was a long silence. Then the little boy's breathless voice came on the line again. " I can't lift her out of the playpen."

OH, if I were rid of this affliction I would embrace the world!" These were the words of that great master of music, Beethoven, when he was struggling with the rapidly-growing problem of deafness. And for years he avoided mixing with people because he found it impossible to admit the cause of his deep despair. But, as so often happens, good came out of bad. His unhappiness gave power to his pen and he went on to write more and more wonderful compositions.

Instead of giving in to thoughts of self-destruction he mastered the handicap that could have overwhelmed him. He worked; he created; he achieved. And the result is the grand, passionate music which we hold as his legacy today. Without a doubt, Beethoven had stupendous talent. But he also had the simpler, precious qualities of courage and determination.

WEDNESDAY—AUGUST 25.

THE members of the village chapel couldn't remember a baby crying so much during a baptism. He just wailed and howled even when the actual baptism was over, and he threatened to disrupt the rest of the service.

He was passed from one to another, but all attempts to pacify him were in vain—until at last he came to Grandma. Almost at once the crying stopped. The calm was so unexpected and so welcome that, after the service was over, the minister congratulated the old lady and asked her the secret.

" Oh," she replied, " I just stuck my finger in his mouth!"

THURSDAY—AUGUST 26.

THIS sign was seen displayed beside some packets of seeds on a stall in a Birmingham market:

French Beans
Not Prize-winners, but Good Runners-up.

Well, isn't that the sort of spirit that we should have, too?

FRIDAY—AUGUST 27.

A READER has sent me these lines which she found in the porch of Wickam Parish Church, Hampshire:

To all who are weary and seek rest:
To all who mourn and long for comfort:
To all who struggle and desire victory:
To all who sin and need a Saviour:
To all who are idle and look for service:
To all who are strangers and want fellowship:
To all who hunger and thirst after
    righteousness:
And to whomsoever will come:

This church has opened wide her doors and, in the name of the Lord Jesus Christ, says, to all of you—WELCOME!

SATURDAY—AUGUST 28.

I CAME across this by the German poet Goëthe the other day, and thought it well worth passing on:

" Every day one should at least hear one little song, read one good poem, contemplate an exquisite painting, and, if it is at all possible, speak a few sensible words."

VARIETY

The trees today look different
To the way they were last week,
And who knows what tomorrow
Will yield to those who seek?
For Nature never lets things stay
But mounts a new show every day!

SUNDAY—AUGUST 29.

BEHOLD, now is the accepted time; behold, now is the day of salvation.

MONDAY—AUGUST 30.

A LITTLE while ago I was reading a book which mentioned the introduction of food rationing in 1940 during the Second World War. It has often been argued that our health was better during those restricted days than when we could eat as much as we liked of anything that we liked. But, of course, there were the inevitable grumbles from some people about not being able to have all that they wanted.

Thinking about this reminded me of a notice I once saw in a grocer's shop during those days of rationing. It said:

" There was no sugar till the 13th century; no coal fires till the 14th century; no buttered bread till the 15th century; no potatoes till the 16th century; no tea and coffee till the 17th century; no puddings till the 18th century; no gas and electricity till the 19th century. So don't grumble!"

A grocer? A philosopher, too!

TUESDAY—AUGUST 31.

SPREAD a little kindness,
Plan a little plot,
Make a bit of sunshine
In some gloomy spot.
That's the way to cheer up
Folk who're feeling sad,
Odd that it will also
Make your own heart glad!

SEPTEMBER

WEDNESDAY—SEPTEMBER 1.

MUMMY was having an argument with five-year-old Shirley.

In a tone of finality, Shirley suddenly said: " Look, Mummy—I ought to know. I go to school, and you don't !"

THURSDAY—SEPTEMBER 2.

ALL the best recipes contain a special extra ingredient. I was reminded of that when I heard about the class of 12-year-olds from Craigroyston High School, in Edinburgh, who visited some old folk at Lamb's House in Leith. The children chatted with the old people who spend the day at this centre, and the senior citizens were delighted to see them.

A few days later, four boys from the class arrived at Lamb's House on their own. Shyly they handed over a gift—four jars of bramble jelly! They explained they'd enjoyed their visit so much, they wanted to do something for their hosts. They'd no money, so they'd gone out and picked brambles.

They'd got the sugar from their mothers and made the jelly all by themselves. Four pounds of bramble jelly between a hundred old people may not sound much, but everyone had a taste. It was delicious !

But that's not surprising. For the bramble jelly contained not just berry juice and sugar, but care and patience, and a bit more than that, the best extra ingredient of all—thoughtfulness.

IDEAL

If I could choose my dwelling place
Nothing would please me more
Then a sheltered nook among green hills
And a stream beside my door.

FRIDAY—SEPTEMBER 3.

MARGARET M. GEMMELL, of Orange, Connecticut, USA, has written many beautiful poems, but here is one to make you smile:

I know a funny little lad
Who, much to my surprise,
When summer comes, and school is out
Is up before sunrise.

But soon as school bell rings again
That drowsy sleepy-head,
No matter what I say or do,
Will not get out of bed!

SATURDAY—SEPTEMBER 4.

WINCHESTER was the seat of the Saxon kings and the ancient capital of England. It also boasts the largest cathedral in England, which in turn has the longest nave in Europe.

During the English Civil War, the Parliamentary soldiers smashed many of the stained-glass windows. Some time later, an unknown workman lovingly gathered up fragments of the broken glass and used them to form a lovely window which is today one of Winchester Cathedral's finest treasures.

Filling the large west window is a reverent mosaic comprising literally hundreds of pieces of ancient stained-glass—as beautiful as the original windows from which the fragments came.

SUNDAY—SEPTEMBER 5.

WATCH ye, stand fast in the faith, quit you like men, be strong.

K

Monday—September 6.

IT had been a long, dry summer and the countryside was parched for lack of rain. The harvest was threatened unless there was some respite in the drought and so serious was the situation that the vicar of a little country parish, where almost everyone's livelihood depended upon the harvest, felt it right to make it known to his parishioners that on the following Sunday prayers would be offered for rain. After all, the Prayer Book made provision for such an emergency: " Send us, we beseech Thee, in this our necessity, such moderate rain and showers that we may receive the fruits of the earth to our comfort . . ."

The following Sunday as the villagers made their way to church in the sunshine only one small girl showed the strength of her faith—she was carrying an umbrella!

Tuesday—September 7.

IN the year 1823 a new opera was staged at Covent Garden Opera House. It was called *Clari, the Maid of Milan,* and was written by an American actor named John Howard Payne, who later became the American consul in Tunis, where there is a memorial to him.

The opera was a complete flop, and has never had another full performance.

But it contained one song which lives on and appeals to every new generation in turn. I don't know what the other songs in that opera were like—they may well have been poor and unmemorable—but John Howard Payne has reached many a heart and drawn many a tear with the evergreen " Home, Sweet Home ".

THE FRIENDSHIP BOOK

I ALMOST phoned, I almost spoke,
I almost invited the next-door-folk:
Oh, what a pity no-one knew
All the good I meant to do!

MARY SHIFFER was brought up in great poverty in Dublin and in 1916 she came to London to seek her fortune. She was taken on as a housemaid at the fashionable Hyde Park Hotel and there she worked until her death sixty years later.

Throughout those years she never occupied anything but a lowly position. How was it then, that when she retired, the hotel management approached Mr Anthony Masters and asked him to write her biography?

Because, humble though her position was, it brought her into contact with such people as the Duke of Windsor, Queen Mary, King George VI, Rudolph Valentino and many other great and famous men and women. She served them in various ways and they came to like and trust the little Irishwoman who in turn knew them better than most of those who served them publicly.

What was her secret? In his book about Mary, Mr Masters tells how he went to visit a retired manager of the hotel. Like Mary, he had been brought up on the poverty line. Unlike Mary he had reached the top of his profession.

"But we had one thing in common," he told Mr Masters. "Neither of us saw any shame in serving. All our lives we served people."

I salute them both, the successful manager and the contented maidservant.

FRIDAY—SEPTEMBER 10.

HAVE you ever come across this delightful tribute to happiness by the Frenchman, Monsieur Aumonier?

" Happiness is to have enough for the day's needs with always some to spare for those who have not.

" It is to possess the love of friends and to have the knowledge that all is well with them.

" It is to live in peace with all men.

" Happiness is to have the strength to face with courage all that the day may bring.

" It is to cherish the gift of laughter, to be quick to note all that is lovely and of good report.

" Happiness is to find our joy in the common things of life—for so will youth abide in our hearts till the end of our days."

SATURDAY—SEPTEMBER 11.

MRS FLORENCE ALLSHORN founded the St Julian's Community, a training centre for Christian workers, near Horsham in Sussex.

In a letter to a friend she wrote this about holidays:

" One of the best things you can do on your holiday is to ask for nothing, want nothing, but in everything praise God."

It's a thought well worth packing along with your toothbrush and pyjamas.

SUNDAY—SEPTEMBER 12.

THOU wilt shew me the path of life: in thy presence is fulness of joy: at thy right hand there are pleasures for evermore.

THE FRIENDSHIP BOOK

WE had a grand sermon yesterday," said my friend Willie to me as I stopped for a word with him while he was sweeping his path one Monday morning.

" ' Look not back,' " said Willie. " I think our minister preaches on that text once every six months. But I don't mind—it's so true."

" I suppose you mean that if we're always looking back to happy days we've had we're not very likely to be happy now?" I asked.

" That's right," said Willie. " The minister summed it up like this: ' If you live entirely in the present you miss the pleasure of anticipation. If you live entirely in the future you're never contented with the present. But if you live entirely in the past you spoil both present and future.' And it's true isn't it?"

SOME years ago a man arrived at a tiny railway station half an hour before his train was due. As he waited he could not help noticing that the stationmaster (who was the whole station staff) was busy all the time. If he was not weeding the plots on the platform he was wielding a broom or giving a polish to the booking office window. He never stopped.

The traveller, somewhat amused by the stationmaster's obvious determination to make his station so spick and span, commented: " Need you work so hard to make your station perfect? It isn't Euston, you know."

" I know that, sir," came the polite reply. " But it's on the same line!"

WEDNESDAY—SEPTEMBER 15.

GENERAL SHERMAN, the Federal hero of the American Civil War, was once the honoured guest at a banquet followed by a reception.

Many people shook hands with him, among them one man whose face seemed familiar but whom he could not place.

" And who are you?" the General murmured as he welcomed the guest.

" Made your shirts, sir," said the man quietly.

" Ah, of course," exclaimed the General, who was a little hard of hearing. Then turning to the assembled guests he said, " Gentlemen, allow me to present my dear friend Major Shurtz!"

THURSDAY—SEPTEMBER 16.

THE man who invented the concertina was a very shy soul, who preferred to work in secret, and who was industrious to the very end of his life. His invention soon became popular in society circles, and playing the concertina was the favourite recreation of at least one British Prime Minister—Arthur James Balfour.

The dulcet strains of the concertina may still be heard today. Travelling showmen throughout Europe, country dancers, and the Salvation Army have all used the concertina to provide their musical accompaniment. Without the concertina we would never have had today's piano-accordions which are based on it.

The man who invented it in 1829 was Charles Wheatstone—better-known perhaps for his work in acoustics and electricity, but to whom we owe the original bellows-blown reed instrument known as the concertina.

THE FRIENDSHIP BOOK

HAVE you ever heard of " The League of the Golden Pen "? It was started many years ago and its members pledged themselves to " Write a letter at least once a month, in the spirit of Christ, to stranger, friend, or kin, to give cheer, courage, or counsel."

Isn't that a lovely thought? It's something we could all do. Why not start today?

MRS. Hibberd is rather a shy, quiet lady . . . definitely not the sort to boast or draw attention to herself. So if my wife had not told me I might never have known about Mrs. Hibberd's artistic talents.

Apparently, she spends most of her evenings crocheting the most delicate and exquisite baby clothes. Several times a year these little garments are parcelled up and sent out to missionaries in Third World countries, who pass them on to the families most in need.

Whenever I think of Mrs. Hibberd now I am reminded of the naturally shy nightingale. We very rarely catch a proper look at this lovely songbird, because it prefers to sing from a hidden perch. But we hear its sweet music, and just knowing it's there in the background makes this old world seem a better place.

THE Lord is my rock, and my fortress, and my deliverer; my God, my strength, in whom I will trust.

THE FRIENDSHIP BOOK

A LADY went to visit her doctor on a very wet day. When he entered his consulting room she commented, " It's a miserable day, doctor!"

With a smile the doctor replied, " When God sends rain, rain's my choice."

I don't know if he gave the woman a prescription for medicine, but he certainly gave her a prescription for contentment.

B ABA AMTE is a high-caste Brahmin who has spent all his life breaking down class barriers and helping poorer folk wherever possible. He never intended getting married, until in 1946 he noticed a girl named Sadhana, from a scholarly family, who was at the time attending the wedding of her elder sister.

During the ceremony, Sadhana slipped out and went into the scullery to wash clothes with an elderly servant woman whom everyone had been scolding. " Don't tell anyone," Sadhana said as she went back to the celebrations.

But Baba Amte had both seen and heard, and before long these two high-born Indians who both believed in crossing class barriers, were married. Ever since, they have worked to rehabilitate and care for victims of leprosy, establishing new settlements at Anandwan, Ashokwan, Somnath, and Hemalkasa, all of which are now prosperous little agricultural villages where before there was only forest and waste land.

Baba Amte says of himself: " I want to be a man who goes round with a little oil-can and, when he sees a breakdown, offers his help."

THE FRIENDSHIP BOOK

A N American poet named Thomas Blake wrote:
Every morning lean thine arms awhile
Upon the window sill of heaven
And gaze upon thy Lord;
Then, with the vision in thy heart,
Turn, strong, to meet thy day.

W ALTER WILKINSON was a travelling Punch and Judy man who not only brought delight to children and adults alike with his traditional show, but captured something of the fascination of his travels, the places he visited and the people he met in a series of intriguing books—*Puppets in Yorkshire, Puppets through Lancashire, Puppets into Scotland,* and others.

He was a philosopher as well as a showman, and much of his philosophy derives from the country characters with whom he had so obvious an affinity. He tells of one autumn, " stormy enough to make outdoor Punch and Judy work a hazard, and camping not too comfortable," when he decided to make for winter quarters.

He writes, " I left the farmer still struggling with his hay in this month of September, and cocking up the drowned stuff for the third time. ' Ah! We want some patience,' he said. ' We must all ha' patience. And if we get no hay this year, happen we will next, or the next after that.'"

Walter Wilkinson commented: " A large view of things, which fitted well with the farm among the wild mountains."

Life might be easier for a lot of us if we could cultivate that largeness of patience and optimism.

CHARLES KINGSLEY once commented: " The men I have seen succeed best in life have always been cheerful and hopeful men."

He certainly embodied his own sentiments. The author of *Westward Ho!* and *The Water Babies* was a typical country parson, honest and kindly, without the least personal ambition, and a great lover of nature. As an active campaigner for social reforms he did not always succeed, but he certainly worked with a will.

Out of his own experience he could say: " Thank God every morning, when you get up, that you have something to do that day, which must be done, whether you like it or not. Being forced to work, and forced to do your best will breed in you temperance and self-control, diligence and strength of will, cheerfulness and content and a hundred virtues which the idle man will never know."

SATURDAY—SEPTEMBER 25.

THE story is told of a man who did not approve of foreign missions. He was visiting a strange church and found to his consternation that it was a missionary service, with a collection for missionary work. When the collector came to him with the plate he whispered, " I never give to missions."

" Then you take something off the plate, sir," whispered the steward. " It's for the heathen!"

SUNDAY—SEPTEMBER 26.

FOR thou wilt light my candle: the Lord my God will enlighten my darkness.

*IT'S nice to think that happiness is just a smile
away,
That gloomy thoughts and ugly moods need never
spoil our day;
If we can learn the simple art of smiling now and
then,
And thinking only pleasant thoughts whilst
counting up to ten;
The world outside will greet us with a wide
infectious grin,
For smiling is contagious and it lets the sunshine
in!*

A FRIEND who has *The Southern Churchman*
magazine posted from Nebraska, sends this
extract: "An 81-year-old lady of Farnam,
Nebraska, who has a great many friends, went into
hospital not long ago. Notwithstanding her age she
takes a deep and personal interest in Matthew's
Mission at Farnam. Before she went to the hospital
she left word that if any of her friends thought of
sending her flowers she would prefer to have them
give the money towards coal to heat the Mission
for the winter."

Before she left the hospital the Mission had
money enough for nearly two winters' coal supply,
and her friends were preparing to welcome her
home with " a shower of coal nuggets."

" Say it with flowers " is often a good way of
expressing sympathy or gratitude but there is a
place too for " Saying it with coal "—or in some
other practical way. How many ways, I wonder,
can we find of " saying it "?

THE CROSSING

" One step at a time "—that's what we were told,
When we were little, but terribly bold.
But wasn't it hard our terror to hide
When steps were so small and spaces so wide!

TOWARDS the end of the Second World War, Wilfred Pickles was told that a young soldier named Robinson wanted to see him. They had met before, and Wilfred Pickles had been so impressed that he had told him he felt he had a future in broadcasting.

Now Robinson, a casualty of Dunkirk, had been invalided home and discharged from the Army. He told Pickles that when he was fit again he hoped to return to his old job of selling boilers, but Wilfred Pickles had other ideas and offered to train him as an announcer. After a few trials, the 21-year-old soldier made a test recording—and was engaged on the spot.

So began a career with the BBC, first as an announcer in Manchester, then as a newsreader and film commentator in London. Since then Robert Robinson has appeared regularly on countless TV and radio programmes and his warm, friendly voice has endeared him to people in all walks of life.

I WONDER if you have heard the story of Abe, a simple soul who did odd jobs for the local blacksmith in a small Yorkshire town. Once he was given an old watch by his employer.

For a few days it kept good time and then, one morning, Abe arrived at the smithy with a long face. " The watch has stopped, Mr Cawthra."

" Then we'd better have a look at it, lad."

Inside they found a small dead fly. Abe's eyes opened wide. " Ee," he said slowly, " no wonder it's stopped—the driver's dead!"

OCTOBER

FRIDAY—OCTOBER 1.

ABOUT a hundred years ago, a thirteen-year-old boy named John Nicholson promised his dying mother that he would read a portion of her Bible every day of his life. John kept that promise for 73 years. He did more than that. He made it possible for many others to do so, too. Some time later, he had to share his hotel bedroom with another traveller, and as he read his Bible, he discovered that his fellow-traveller was a Christian too. They had such a happy time together that they decided to start an association of Christian travelling men with an emblem whereby they could recognise each other.

For over seventy years the association founded by John Nicholson and his friend has been responsible for placing copies of the Scriptures in hotel rooms, hospitals, schools and prisons. Their name is Gideons International, and their symbol is a two-handled pitcher and torch commemorating the story of Gideon's victory over the Midianites, as described in the Book of Judges.

SATURDAY—OCTOBER 2.

THAT great artist, Van Gogh, often suffered from feelings of despair. There were many times, he said, when he felt like a bird trapped in a cage.

" And do you know what takes away the cage?" he wrote. " Brotherhood, friendship, love. They open the cage like a magic key. He who creates sympathy, creates life."

THE FRIENDSHIP BOOK

L ORD, lift thou up the light of thy countenance upon us.

T WO hundred years ago Robin Lawless was a bookseller in the Soho district of London. Once in his youth he applied to his employer " for a lowering of wages as our previous year's takings were not so good."

That's all I have to tell you about him. But isn't it enough? Two hundred years later that single incident lives on after him.

I ASKED the Lady of the House what she would like for her birthday and she said she would like a polished stone pendant. So, off we went to visit a lapidary shop that had a big selection of stones.

While I was waiting I glanced round the shop and was attracted by a piece of rock that had been sawn in two. The outside had nothing to commend it, just a dull, grey surface, but the inside was completely different. A light shone on beautiful amethyst crystals of delicate beauty.

When the Lady of the House had made her choice I drew her attention to the section of rock. " Well, of course," she said. " Many rocks are like people, who may look dull and uninteresting on the outside—you've got to get to know them to find the beauty locked away inside."

It was quite a lesson to pick up on a simple shopping trip!

THE FRIENDSHIP BOOK

A YOUNG politician was constantly interrupted as he tried to deliver a carefully prepared election speech.

When it was over he left the platform complaining bitterly. An experienced colleague rebuked him. " You should be grateful," he said. " The person who never interrupts probably isn't listening to you!"

B EFORE he became the Provost of Bradford, the Rev. Brandon Jackson was the vicar of St Peter's, three miles away in Shipley. Once he found out that a local milkman had not had a holiday with his wife for several years.

Brandon Jackson took over the milk-round himself for a week. In addition to his normal church duties, he set off on the milk-round at crack of dawn every morning. I don't know how many pints he put on the wrong doorsteps, but he certainly showed that his heart was in the right place!

T HE preacher I heard last Sunday had one great virtue. He used few words, and yet he said so much. There is great value, as well as great discipline, in saying something briefly. It is the art of the postcard rather than the letter.

After all, Jesus gave us his greatest commandment in three words: " Love one another." And his greatest promise in five words: " I am with you always."

THE FRIENDSHIP BOOK

I CAME across these " Reasons For Living " the other day. I don't know who wrote them, but they surely have a message for us:

Is anybody happier
Because you passed this way?
Does anyone remember
That you spoke to them today?
The day is almost over,
And its toiling time is through,
Is there anyone to utter
Now a kindly word of you?

Can you say tonight in parting
With the day that's slipping fast,
That you helped a single brother
Of the many that you passed?
Is a single heart rejoicing
Over what you did or said?
Does the man whose hopes were fading,
Now with courage look ahead?

Did you waste the day, or lose it?
Was it well or sorely spent?
Did you leave a trail of kindness,
Or a scar of discontent?
As you close your eyes in slumber,
Do you think that God will say
" You have earned one more tomorrow
By the work you did today "?

THEREFORE hath the Lord recompensed me according to my righteousness, according to the cleanness of my hands in his eyesight.

L

THE FRIENDSHIP BOOK

LAURENCE OLIVIER once said of his own acting, " I've got an awful way of flinging my hands about, which I detest, and I try to control it. But sometimes a part requires all you've got, weaknesses and all, and I just let myself go; I let it all happen and hope for the best."

Not a bad prescription for life—to give it all we've got, weaknesses and all.

THE Lady of the House and I were looking through an old family photograph album, and I suppose it ought to have been obvious to us before but we were struck by the fact that the photos were, without exception, of pleasant places, happy occasions and smiling people. They were photos of holidays and weddings, of children playing on the beach and paddling in the sea, of laughing family groups, of the beautiful gardens of stately homes, of mountains and rivers.

There were none of crying children, or smoky mill chimneys or slag heaps, or road accidents we had passed on the motorway—nothing like that.

" Well, of course not," you will say. " Those are not the kind of pictures we store up in our albums."

Yet, if we think of our memories as rather like photograph albums, what a lot of odd pictures we often store up there—disappointments and frustrations, the unkind things people have said and done, sad experiences and things best forgotten.

We love browsing over our photograph album. Memory-browsing ought to be just as pleasant.

WEDNESDAY—OCTOBER 13.

HE who has a thousand friends
Has not a friend to spare;
And he who has one enemy
Shall meet him everywhere.

A friend sent me the above lines which I in turn am passing on to you. She says it was written by one Ali Ben Abu Taleb in Arabia, many centuries ago. But it's still as apt now as I am sure it was then. Some things *never* change, do they?

THURSDAY—OCTOBER 14.

THE late Arturo Toscanini, one time musical director of La Scala, Milan, once conducted a concert by a leading American orchestra. The music was broadcast through radio stations all over the States. At the end of one of the items the announcer said: " We have received a letter from a shepherd in Wyoming who tells us, 'My only entertainment is a battery radio and my fiddle, which I play a great deal. I have lost the tuning of my A string. Please, sir, would you sound the note A on your programme this week, so that I can tune my fiddle?' "

On hearing this, the great Toscanini raised his baton and requested his musicians to sound the note A. And as the note sounded throughout America, that lonely shepherd in Wyoming tuned his fiddle and began to play.

Many people are out of tune with life, discordant in their relationships with others and at odds with themselves. How worth while if, by some simple act of kindness or consideration, we can help such a one to find a more harmonious way of living.

FRIDAY—OCTOBER 15.

IN one of his letters to his friend Robert Lloyd, Charles Lamb wrote: " You say that ' this world to you seems drained of all its sweets!' At first I had hoped you only meant to intimate the high price of sugar, but I am afraid you meant more. O, Robert, I don't know what you call sweet. Honey and the honeycomb, roses and violets are yet in the earth. The sun and moon yet reign in heaven, and the lesser lights keep up their pretty twinklings. Meats and drink, sweet sights and sweet smells, a country walk, spring and autumn, follies and repentance, quarrels and reconcilements, have all a sweetness by turns.

" Good humour and good nature, friends at home that love you, and friends abroad that miss you—you possess all these things, and more innumerable, and these are all sweet things. You may extract honey from everything."

Those words were written, remember, by a man whose own life had more than its share of sadness and tragedy, yet, like George Borrow, he could say, " Life is sweet, brother!" And so may we—if we will.

SATURDAY—OCTOBER 16.

THE founder of the Promenade Concerts, Sir Henry Wood, once gave this advice to young conductors concerning rehearsals: " If things go badly, don't get ruffled; keep calm and keep cheerful above all. It's the only sure way of obtaining the response from your players which the music deserves."

Good advice for conductors—or for anyone learning how to conduct his own life.

SUNDAY—OCTOBER 17.

AND the angel of the Lord appeared unto him in a flame of fire out of the midst of the bush: and he looked, and behold, the bush burned with fire, and the bush was not consumed.

MONDAY—OCTOBER 18.

A COUNTRY vicar one day asked an aged villager, " How is it that I haven't seen you at church lately?"

Came the honest reply: " I ain't been, sir!"

TUESDAY—OCTOBER 19.

THIS poem came to me in an envelope with no name and no address. I suppose the sender felt the verses spoke for themselves—and I thoroughly agree.

The thing that goes the furthest toward making life worth while,
That costs the least and does the most is just a pleasing smile;
The smile that bubbles from the heart, that loves its fellow-men,
Will drive away the clouds and gloom, and coax the sun again.

There is no room for sadness when we see a cheery smile,
It always has the same good luck, it's never out of style,
It nerves us on to try again when failure makes us blue,
The dimples of encouragement are good for me and you.

THE FRIENDSHIP BOOK

L OVING is giving,
We all know that's true.
So here for a start
Is something to do—
Look outward, not inward,
In each passing day;
And the joy you give others
Will soon come your way.

TOM MORGAN was a highly respected farmer in Wales and a member of the local village council. Everyone agreed that he had the interests of all the villagers at heart and though he lacked formal education his wise advice on local affairs was eagerly sought and appreciated. In the words of a distinguished Member of Parliament who knew him well, Tom was "one of Nature's true gentlemen."

One evening, the village council was holding its quarterly meeting. The local squire was in the chair and throughout the proceedings he clearly showed, as in the past, his hostility to the farmer. The latter put forward various practical schemes which would in his opinion greatly improve the village amenities.

The chairman disagreed with them all, at last bursting out angrily, "Absolute rubbish! Listen, Morgan, I am a knowledgeable man, and I would have you understand that I have had degrees conferred on me by three different universities!"

Tom bowed politely and remarked, "It's a great pity, sir, that one of them was not for good manners."

THE FRIENDSHIP BOOK

AN Indian legend tells of a beggar who sat with his bowl containing a handful of rice, waiting hopefully for the passing of the Rajah's procession, hoping that some nobleman might put a coin in the bowl. To his astonishment the Rajah stopped directly by him and asked him what he wanted.

" Alms!" cried the beggar in confusion.

" Give me something first," said the Rajah.

Give to the Rajah, who had everything? Angrily the beggar threw a single grain of rice at him. Then, as he looked in his bowl, he saw a tiny piece of gold, as big as a single grain of rice.

" Fool that I am!" cried the beggar. " Why did I not give him it all?"

" He who sows sparingly shall reap sparingly " is true, not simply in a material sense, but true of friendship, love, sympathy, encouragement and all that it is in our power to give.

I LIKE a nice cup of tea in the morning, And a nice cup of tea for my tea . . ."

So goes the old music-hall song, and how true it is! Two hundred years ago this standard beverage was still something of a novelty, but now it has become " the cup that cheers," and a token of friendship.

How often we sit down to chat over " a nice cup of tea." And if anyone is upset or in trouble, the first thing we do is put the kettle on. Tea was once an expensive oriental luxury; now it is comparatively cheap. But let us never take it for granted! For most of us life would be quite unthinkable without a cup of tea.

I WONDER!

The world was full of wonders
When we were very young;
And How? and When? and Why? and What?
Were always on our tongue.

Time makes us old and wiser,
  But as the years slip by
How happy still to see the world
  Through childhood's eager eye.

THE FRIENDSHIP BOOK

LET the words of my mouth, and the meditation of my heart, be acceptable in thy sight, O Lord, my strength, and my redeemer.

WHEN in the early years of this century, a Canadian-born doctor, Sir William Osler, visited a children's ward, he noticed one little girl who sat forlornly on the edge of her bed, alone, clutching a cheap wooden doll, ignored by the other children.

The great physician looked at the crumpled figure, then questioningly at the ward nurse. "We've tried to get Jenny to play," the nurse whispered. "But no one comes to see her. Her mother is dead and her father is a sailor. The children have a strange code. If you don't have any visitors, you're ignored."

Sir William walked over to the child's bed. "May I sit down, please?" he asked. The girl's face lit up. "I can't stay very long this time," he went on, in a voice loud enough for the others to hear. "But I've wanted to see you so badly."

For five minutes he sat talking with her, asking about her doll's health and solemnly pulling out his stethoscope to listen to the doll's chest.

As he left, he turned to the youngster with a twinkle in his eyes. "Now you won't forget our secret, will you?" he asked in a carrying voice. "And mind, don't tell a soul!"

At the door, he looked back. His new friend was now at the centre of a curious, respectful throng. From that moment Jenny had no lack of friends.

THE FRIENDSHIP BOOK

A YOUNG couple wishing to have a talk about their approaching wedding, were ushered into the minister's study and they were discussing the order of the marriage service when the young couple requested a slight change in the wording.

" What are the words you wish to change?" asked the minister.

The couple said, " Instead of ' till death us do part ', may we have ' for ever and ever '?"

And so the wedding was celebrated, and the two young people plighted their troth to each other " for ever and ever ".

I think it's a rather lovely idea.

A FRIEND of mine boarded a crowded, pay-as-you-enter bus one dull, rainy day. He joined the weary workers and laden shoppers, all jostling for seats. Suddenly the driver gave a cheery shout at the top of his voice: " Plenty room upstairs!"

There was a moment's complete silence, and then everybody started to laugh.

It was a single-decker bus!

A YOUNG guide was showing some visitors around the caves at Valkenburg in Holland and drew their attention to the echoes which can be heard in certain parts. He might have explained to them that echoes are caused by reflected sounds. Instead he chose to give his visitors this advice, " Speak kind words," he said, " and you will hear kind echoes."

FRIDAY—OCTOBER 29.

O N a memorial tablet to a certain missionary on
the Pacific island of Tanna is the following
remarkable inscription: " When he landed in 1848
there were no Christians here—and when he left in
1872 there were no heathens."

The missionary was a Scot, John Gibson
Paton, who is still fondly remembered in the New
Hebrides.

Many years later, when some Communists
arrived and tried to tell the islanders that there is
no God, the native Chief replied, " You ought to
thank God, in whose existence you do not believe,
that you came here *after* Paton. He taught us to
have faith and love. If you had come here first, we
would have eaten you!"

SATURDAY—OCTOBER 30.

C HARLES M. SCHWAB was philanthropist
Andrew Carnegie's right-hand man. He had
the great knack of getting on with people, and
when he died, Carnegie had his tombstone
inscribed with these words: " Here lies one who
knew how to get around him men who were
cleverer than himself."

What was Schwab's secret? He once said:
" The way to develop the best that is in a man is
by appreciation. Nothing so kills the ambition of a
man as criticism from his superiors. So I am
anxious to praise—but loth to find fault."

SUNDAY—OCTOBER 31.

H OLD up my goings in thy paths, that my
footsteps slip not.

NOVEMBER

MONDAY—NOVEMBER 1.

THERE isn't much point in nursing a grudge,
 For the one who will suffer is you;
It clouds all the sunbeams that make life worth
  while.
 And blights every happiness, too.
So bury it deep as you possibly can,
 Dig with a smile on your face,
And you'll find where that grudge used to
  rankle and burn,
 A flower will grow in its place.

TUESDAY—NOVEMBER 2.

THERE was once a little boy called Benedict.
 Born in Nursia, Italy, he had rich parents who were able to offer him the best of everything. Benedict, however, had no desire for the good things of life. For him, wealth spelled evil. He was just fourteen when he decided to renounce money and earthly pleasures. He went to live in a cave where for three years he led a Spartan life of meditation and prayer.

 Benedict went on to form religious communities and to establish the great monastery of Monte Cassino. The monks who followed his pattern took vows of chastity and obedience. But they also promised to work hard—for at least seven hours a day—as Benedict's motto was *Laborare est orare* (to work is to pray). His example is still followed by monks of different orders besides the Benedictines who proudly bear his name.

THE FRIENDSHIP BOOK

I'VE often said that I'm not to be drawn into arguments about Women's Lib.

So you can take what you like from this little exchange.

A bachelor and a married man had been discussing the subject.

" If we don't watch out," said the bachelor, " women will be running the world at the end of the century."

The married man only cocked an eyebrow. " Still?" he said.

MANY schools and societies have a motto that they try to live by. A challenging but lovely one was once adopted by a class at Westoning County School, in Bedfordshire:

It is a good heart that says no ill,
but a better heart that thinks none.

WHAT a wonderful thing is prayer! Dr Alexis Carrel has written, " As a physician, I have seen men, after all other therapy had failed, lifted out of disease and melancholy by the serene effort of prayer. It is the only power in the world that seems to overcome the so-called ' laws of nature '. The occasions on which prayer has dramatically done this have been termed ' miracles '. But a constant, quieter miracle takes place hourly in the hearts of men and women who have discovered that prayer supplies them with a steady flow of sustaining power in their daily lives."

THE FRIENDSHIP BOOK

THESE lines, titled *I Do It Unto Thee,* are said to have been written by a young girl in domestic service in England in 1928.

> *Lord of all pots and pans and things,*
> *Since I have no time to be*
> *A saint by doing lovely things,*
> *Or watching late with Thee,*
> *Or dreaming in the dawnlight*
> *Or storming Heaven's gates,*
> *Make me a saint by getting*
> *Meals and washing up the plates.*
>
> *Although I must have Martha's hands,*
> *I have a Mary mind*
> *And when I black the boots and shoes,*
> *Thy sandals, Lord, I find.*
> *I think of how they trod the earth,*
> *What time I scrub the floor.*
> *Accept this meditation, Lord,*
> *I haven't time for more.*
>
> *Warm all the kitchen with Thy love,*
> *And light it with Thy peace,*
> *Forgive me all my worrying*
> *And make all grumbling cease.*
> *Thou who didst love to give men food,*
> *In room, or by the sea,*
> *Accept this service that I do . . .*
> *I do it unto Thee.*

THE statutes of the Lord are right, rejoicing the heart: the commandment of the Lord is pure, enlightening the eyes.

THE FRIENDSHIP BOOK

WITHOUT being arrogant or conceited most of us like to feel we " count for something ". It is the loss of that sense which leads to frustration and despair. Jesus realised this when He assured people that they " counted with God ". " The very hairs of your head are all numbered," He said.

As far as counting with other people is concerned, I have always been very impressed by Robert Louis Stevenson's words: " So long as we are loved by others, I would almost say that we are indispensible; and no man is useless while he has a friend."

Does anyone love us? Have we friends? Then indeed we " count "!

JANE HATCHER is an architectural historian. She loves old buildings—writes, talks and lectures about them. Particularly she delights in old watermills, so many of which have been restored in recent years. But until recently she had never *listened* to one. Then one day, when she was visiting a mill in operation, a man said to her, " Don't these watermills make a lovely noise?"

" I'd never noticed it before," says Jane. " But they do. It's one of the pleasures I had been missing."

It doesn't much matter whether we live in town or country—it's always worth listening for pleasant sounds, for sounds which, perhaps, we have never noticed before. For, when the ear is gladdened, the heart is gladdened too. How many sounds can you discover today which delight the ear?

WEDNESDAY—NOVEMBER 10.

IT'S hard to smile when you feel lost,
It's harder still to laugh.
But smiling makes the shadows go,
And mirth can smooth your path.

So, don't give up, keep plodding on,
You'll find the right connection.
We need to lose our way, at times,
To choose the best direction.

THURSDAY—NOVEMBER 11.

DURING the First World War some soldiers took cover in a trench. Between their trench and that of the enemy, a soldier lay wounded. One soldier begged his officer to allow him to run out of the trench and carry back his fallen friend.

The officer was displeased. He had lost many men and he suspected that the wounded man was beyond help.

" What good would it do?" the officer asked. " You might throw away your own life."

The soldier continued to plead until the officer agreed. Then, bravely, the soldier sprang from the trench and some minutes later reappeared dragging his friend with him.

The officer examined the man and then turned angrily to his soldier. " I told you it wasn't worth the risk. He's dead."

" It *was* worth it," the soldier replied. " He wasn't quite dead when I reached him and he said something important."

Although the wounded man had been in great pain, he had opened his eyes briefly, looked at his friend and said, " I knew you'd come."

M

FRIDAY—NOVEMBER 12.

I WILL never forget the words of a clergyman who was preaching one Remembrance Sunday about courage and how the freedom we enjoy was bought by the courage of ordinary men and women.

"These brave men and women," he said, "were not born courageous. *Courage is fear that has said its prayers.*"

SATURDAY—NOVEMBER 13.

IN November, 1931, Thomas Brooks was elected Mayor of Bethnal Green in London's East End. During his Mayoral year he was decribed as the most contented and happiest man in the borough—easy-going, but firm when required. And if there was any trouble, he would make a clean sweep of it—in more ways than one, for he was a chimney-sweep like his father before him. Thomas Brooks is believed to have been the first chimney-sweep in England to become a Chief Citizen. He was always proud of the fact, and the handle of a sweep's broom over his doorway proclaimed his trade.

One day he was invited to a Garden Party at Buckingham Palace. His day began like any other day—a round of sweeping chimneys, followed by a bath and change for the royal occasion. As soon as the Garden Party was over, he returned to Bethnal Green, got back into working clothes and did one or two more chimneys before finishing for the day.

I have seen a photograph of the Mayor of Bethnal Green, starting out on his daily round as a chimney-sweep. On his face is the smile of a happy and contented man.

SUNDAY—NOVEMBER 14.

AND God shall wipe away all tears from their eyes; and there shall be no more death, neither sorrow, nor crying, neither shall there be any more pain.

MONDAY—NOVEMBER 15.

FOR twenty-six years Ernest Askwith was pastor of a little church in the picturesque village of Robin Hood's Bay in Yorkshire. This period included World War II when he acted as Billeting Officer for evacuees from bomb-threatened cities. He told of one cheerful youngster who, being interviewed by the reception committee, stared hard at them and then said, " You seem a decent lot of folk. Perhaps I could have brought me watch after all!"

TUESDAY—NOVEMBER 16.

I WAS sitting behind the two women on a crowded bus, so I could not help but overhear part of their conversation when they were discussing a mutual friend, whom I'll just call Mrs X. The first woman obviously enjoyed a bit of gossip, and with great relish she began to list all the shortcomings of the absent lady.

The second woman listened quietly for a while, then with a sweet smile on her face, she said, " It's really strange that you should have such a wrong impression of Mrs X. *She* always says nice kind things about *you!*"

I got off at the next stop so I don't know what they spoke about next—but somehow I don't think there would be any more gossip!

WEDNESDAY—NOVEMBER 17.

A LOCAL church was organising a Self-denial Week and members were asked to make some sacrifice and give the money saved to the church. Father said he would stop smoking, Mum that she would do without chocolates for a week, and their elder daughter said she would forgo her usual visit to the cinema.

The young son of the family thought for a moment or two and then said, " I'll give up rice pudding. I never did like the stuff anyhow!" I rather think he missed the point, somehow.

And what a lot we miss, too, if we have never known the satisfaction which comes from true self denial! David Livingstone once said, " I never use the word sacrifice because what people call sacrifice is to me real joy."

THURSDAY—NOVEMBER 18.

WHEN we heard that force twelve gales were hitting the Cornish coast the Lady of the House and I were rather worried about Kathleen, an elderly friend of ours, who lives down there in a remote cottage surrounded by high trees. So you can imagine our relief when we got a letter from her after it was all over telling us that the only damage was a broken greenhouse window and some missing roof slates. " The trees did not give way, even though the strength of the wind was terrible," she wrote. " I watched them from my window. They bent over and this saved them from breaking."

What these trees did naturally, we can do too. Learn to bend a little and you can survive any storm.

FRIDAY—NOVEMBER 19.

A FEW years ago the central tower of the magnificent York Minster was in danger of collapse through the ravages of time, weather and traffic vibration. A great restoration scheme was started and work went on continuously for five years. During the whole of that time there were only three or four days when it was impossible to hold Evensong.

Each afternoon at precisely four o'clock the sound of hammers and pneumatic drills ceased and the choir procession wound its way beneath the scaffolding for the service. A visitor from Australia called it " the four o'clock miracle ".

I know someone who, every night when the local church clock strikes eleven, stops whatever he is doing and spends a few moments in quiet meditation, remembering the blessings of the day, the members of his scattered family, and anyone he knows to be in special need. That is his " eleven o'clock miracle ".

The time of day doesn't matter, but what a lot of difference it can make if we can escape for a few moments from the noise and bustle of our world and discover the healing power of silence.

SATURDAY—NOVEMBER 20.

A TEACHER asked her pupils to make up a list of eleven great men.

As the class was busy writing, she walked between the desks, and noticed one little lad chewing the end of his pen. " Have you finished?" she asked quietly.

" Not quite, Miss," came the reply. " I'm trying to decide on the goalkeeper."

TWO IN HARMONY

I love to play the clarinet
To please my prima donna pet!

YEA, though I walk through the valley of the shadow of death, I will fear no evil: for thou art with me: thy rod and thy staff they comfort me.

MONDAY—NOVEMBER 22.

WHEN we retort, " That's ancient history!" we usually say it a bit contemptuously, but real ancient history (and some of its heroes) have a great deal to teach us. I remember only vaguely from my school-days the details of the great Battle of Thermopylae, but I shall never forget the reply of Dieneces when he was told, " The number of the barbarians is so great that when they shoot their arrows the sun will be darkened."

His answer was, " So much the better; we shall then fight in the shade!" It is not so much the difficulties and dangers we have to face but the attitude in which we face them that determines the quality of our life.

TUESDAY—NOVEMBER 23.

EVERYONE knows how King Alfred forgot to take the cakes out of the oven on time. Not so well known is that he made up for it later when he vowed that if his kingdom was restored he would spend a third of the remainder of his life in serving God. He measured eight hours each day with candles which each burned for four hours. He put the candles in cases of horn scraped until they were thin enough to be transparent. In their cases the candles would not burn too fast from draughts.

He may have forgotten the cakes but, more important, he remembered to find time for God.

WHEN Annunzio Paolo Mantovani, known to music lovers simply as Mantovani, died in March 1980, the newspapers told of his virtuosity on the violin and of his famous concert orchestra with its " tumbling strings ". Much was said of his many famous recordings like " Charmaine " and " Moulin Rouge ".

No mention was made of another quality which endeared him to thousands—his modesty. Fame and success had not changed him. To the public he was Mantovani, but to his fellow musicians he was known affectionately as " Monty " and he would never have wished it otherwise.

THIS story came to me from a friend in America. A little girl was travelling with her family on one of those long sleeper trains they have over there. When night came she was put in the upper bunk, and told that God would look after her. As everyone began to doze off the little girl got a bit frightened, and called out, " Mummy, are you there?"

" Yes, dear," replied her mother.

A little later she called, " Daddy, are you there?"

" Yes, dear," came the reply.

This was repeated several times, until at last another passenger lost patience, and said: " We're all here! Your father, your mother, your brothers and sisters. NOW GO TO SLEEP!"

Silence ruled for several minutes—and then the child was heard to whisper, " Mother—was that God?"

DR NORMAN VINCENT PEALE'S books — among them *The Power of Positive Thinking*—have helped thousands of people to happier and more successful living. He loves to tell the story of how he was once sitting in the co-pilot's seat in an aeroplane in a typhoon area of the Far East, while the pilot was explaining to him the problems of flying in such conditions.

" So what do you do," asked Dr Peale, " when you come across a typhoon?"

" Well," said the pilot, " I don't try to buck it. I just get on its edge and fly the way it's going. That way I turn the typhoon into a tail wind."

Life has its typhoons too, but if we learn how to use them we can turn our difficulties into the means of developing faith and hope and courage. Let your typhoons be tail winds!

SOME friends of mine were reminiscing about their early lives and holidays and fell to wondering why the past often seems more glorious and happy than the present.

They all had their opinions as to why this should be, but one hit the nail on the head when he said, " The reason is that we do not really remember days—we remember moments."

Enjoy life's happy moments and you will remember them as happy days.

FROM the rising of the sun unto the going down of the same the Lord's name is to be praised.

THE FRIENDSHIP BOOK

A S we sat having our bed-time drink and cream crackers, I was listening to a record and the Lady of the House was reading a historical novel. Suddenly she laughed aloud and I looked up questioningly.

" You'll hardly believe it, Francis," she said, " but you know this story is about the ' Hungry 'Forties ', and just then I found myself scraping some of the butter off my biscuit thinking that I must go easy with it during the shortages!"

It is a pretty good tribute to a writer when he or she can get a reader so involved in the story. I suppose this is what sympathy means—" feeling with ", putting ourselves in other people's situations, looking at things from their point of view. Of course we cannot carry everyone's troubles as if they were our own or life would be unbearable but I am sure there is always room in this world for genuine sympathy.

T HESE lines come to me from a young Glasgow mother and she calls it simply " A Mother's Prayer."

Oh, God, you know I'm busy each moment of the day; please help me to remember that I still have time to pray. While I'm washing up the dishes or working at the sink, when I give my babe his bottle, let me use the time to think.

Grant me patience and good humour, contentment with my lot; help me show by my example what I'd like my children taught. Help me make a happy home, the way a home should be; wherein the trust of all of us remains secure in Thee.

DECEMBER

WEDNESDAY—DECEMBER 1.

IN his book *On Being A Real Person*, Dr Harry Emerson Fosdick describes the features of Central Park, New York. He tells how the landscape architects did not try to eliminate the out-cropping rock ledges they encountered but incorporated them in their scheme and so made a park not so much despite them as by means of them.

Then he comments, " Life is a landscaping job. We are handed a site, ample or small, rugged or flat, picturesque or commonplace, whose general outlines or contours are largely determined for us. These basic elements are to be accepted, never as humiliations, commonly as limitations, but most of all as opportunities and even as incentives."

It's an inspiring thought, that the rough and unpromising elements in our lives can be " landscaped " into something useful and beautiful.

THURSDAY—DECEMBER 2.

THAT great preacher, Peter Marshall, gave his congregation this advice, to help them with their Christmas shopping:

" Maybe there's nothing in the shops that your friends and relations need. But what about some token of love—what about love itself, and friendship, and understanding, and consideration, and a helping hand, and a smile and a prayer? You can't buy these things in any shop but these are the things people need. Blessed will they be who receive them this Christmas."

JOYCE MAXTONE GRAHAM is better known to thousands of readers as Jan Struther, author of *Mrs Miniver*, the delightful story of family life during the Second World War. She also wrote a number of popular hymns, including the well-known " Lord of all hopefulness, Lord of all joy."

But here is a thought of hers which deserves to be more widely-known: " Speech may sometimes do harm, but so may silence, and a worse harm at that. No insult ever offered has caused so deep a wound as a tenderness expected and witheld; and no spoken indiscretion was ever so bitterly regretted as the words one did not speak."

What a marvellous ministry even the least of us can exercise by a word of appreciation, help or encouragement!

MARGARET M. GEMMELL sent me this lovely poem which she wrote and called " Crown of the Year ":

> *Passes April's gentle rain,*
> *Too fleeting Maytime's flowering,*
> *Gone is June's rose blush again,*
> *And dark November's glowering.*
>
> *The still warm calm of August breaks,*
> *Bedimmed September's glory,*
> *But for its crown December takes*
> *The old, old Christmas story.*
>
> *And through the year it shines a light*
> *On every heart—sweet Christmas night.*

OH, BROTHER!

*It's Christmas—the time of goodwill—so a chappie
Must do what's expected to keep those girls happy.*

THE FRIENDSHIP BOOK

I WILL declare thy name unto my brethren: in the midst of the congregation will I praise thee.

IT was a cold winter's night and Mrs Miller had just come out of hospital. It was lovely to be at her own fireside again and she was happy just to sit in the glow of the flames.

Then the bell rang and standing at the door was a message boy holding out a lovely azalea. Eagerly she looked at the small card attached to the wrapping. It said simply: " With good wishes and deep gratitude from J.C.C."

Now, J.C.C. was one of the best-liked shopkeepers in the town. But why, she wondered, had he sent her such a generous gift? It was several days later before she was able to thank him.

" Well, I heard you had been in hospital," he said. " I just wanted you to know that I still remembered all that you did for me."

Eight years ago, he had been at the worst stage of what is now known as " a drink problem." His friends had begun to shun him and his business was near ruin. Many a night she had seen him in the street and had helped him to his home while others crossed the street to avoid him. And it was she who had quietly persuaded him to take the course of treatment that reshaped his life.

Mrs Miller could only stammer out: " But I did nothing, really."

" You did everything," he said. " And I can't forget it. You didn't know me well, but you were a better friend to me than my friends."

THE FRIENDSHIP BOOK

R EMEMBER, though the past is past,
 Today remains today.
The future, though unknown to us,
 Is not so far away.
The promise of tomorrow
 Is a challenge we must meet.
Good luck, brave heart, and courage show,
 Each new day that you greet.

G REAT men and women often earn impressive obituaries tracing their careers and achievements. The nicest obituaries, however, are often the simplest. Like that of a retired clergyman which appeared in a church magazine. It said, " Nobody feared him, many loved him, and he was especially gentle with young children."

W E all associate mince pies with Christmas, but do you know why? Apparently in the 14th century mince pies were oval or cradle-shaped, like a manger, and often had on them the baby Jesus outlined on the pastry. The filling was made with game, poultry, beef, eggs and spices. They were cooked to remind people of the manger in which Jesus was born, and were eaten quickly while people thought about the Holy Child.

Today some of us make a silent wish when we take our first bite of a mince pie. It may sound a little superstitious but it helps to remind us of the origin of mince pies and of the real meaning of Christmas.

FRIDAY—DECEMBER 10.

ONE of our local worthies was celebrating his ninety-ninth birthday and was visited by many well-wishers bringing their greetings and presents. Among the visitors was a young reporter from the district newspaper.

" Congratulations, sir," he said. " I hope I shall have the privilege of being here when you celebrate your hundredth birthday."

The old man looked him up and down and then said, " Well, I don't see why not. You look healthy enough!"

SATURDAY—DECEMBER 11.

DR. John Wilson who years ago conducted an influential ministry in a poor area of Woolwich used to tell a story of a fellow-minister who was leading his people in the building of a new church. He was anxious that it should be opened free from debt, so appeals were made for gifts throughout the district.

A small boy from a poor family who was in the Sunday School wrote: " Dear minister, I am glad that you are building a new church and want it to be opened without any debt, so I am sending one penny towards the cost.

Yours truly, Johnny."

Then he wrote at the bottom: " P.S. If you want any more, let me know."

Johnny had the right spirit!

SUNDAY—DECEMBER 12.

BECAUSE he hath inclined his ear unto me, therefore will I call upon him as long as I live.

WITNESS

The wind's wild music in the trees,
    The gorgeous canvas of the sky—
Nature in every mood can please
    The listening ear, the seeing eye.
And we can savour day by day
Her infinite variety.

MONDAY—DECEMBER 13.

FOR 28 years the late Victor Silvester, the bandleader who brought strict tempo to ballroom dancing, had a weekly radio programme on the BBC World Service.

Victor Silvester's " slow, slow, quick, quick, slow ", reached people over the air in many unlikely places. In 1972, a man captured by terrorists in Buenos Aires wrote to the BBC after his release, saying that during the many weeks of his captivity he had been allowed a radio and that it was Victor's music and gentle reassuring voice that had consoled him most.

Victor also possessed a sense of humour. One cold day he introduced his programme with a " weather report " from London. He said that outside the studio the weather was " Snow, snow, thick, thick, snow "!

TUESDAY—DECEMBER 14.

A MISSIONARY in the Balkans once took a party of boys from a village down in a valley on an expedition to the top of a mountain for the first time. On the summit one of them looked wonderingly around, first in one direction and then in another. Finally, he said incredulously, " What a wonderful world! I never dreamed it was so large!"

Horizons widen for us when we stand on the heights—and that doesn't necessarily mean climbing a mountain. A book, a piece of music, a visit to a great cathedral or an ancient castle, a fresh hobby, a new friendship—these are but a few of the ways in which we can, so to speak, " stand on the heights " and discover that life has a larger dimension than we dreamed.

THE FRIENDSHIP BOOK

I LOVE to come home when the Lady of the House has been baking bread and the house is filled with its delicious smell. Fresh, crusty bread. Other foods may pall, but never bread.

I remember a business friend of mine who told me that one Christmas he had to attend eight business lunches in a row. After all that, he was looking for some good plain fair.

Of course, we could not live on bread alone, but it is a reminder to us that we tire of the luxuries more quickly than of the simple, basic necessities. And it's true not only of food. We might all benefit by taking to heart Rudyard Kipling's prayer, "Teach us delight in simple things."

NO wonder the teacher smiled—
He'd taken a party of schoolchildren from Edinburgh for a week's hill-walking and nature study in the Cairngorms.

After they'd settled down in their camp site, he told them he'd make a trip to Aviemore. If anyone wanted a letter posted, he'd take it down.

One boy said he'd promised to send his mother a postcard, but when he made no move to write one, the teacher told him he'd have to hurry.

" I'll not be a second," said the boy. Diving into his rucksack he brought out a neatly written and addressed postcard, already stamped. With a smile he showed it to the teacher.

Written by his mother before he left home, it read—" Dear Mum, Have arrived safely. Hope you're well. Love, Andrew."

A mum who knows what boys are like!

FRIDAY—DECEMBER 17.

IN one of his books, writing about education, Aldous Huxley says, " It doesn't much matter what you teach the little beggars as long as it is something they don't like!" Well, perhaps that is a bit over-cynical and I don't suppose the educational psychologists would agree with it.

Yet we know, if we are honest, that it has often been the hard experiences in our lives that have developed our characters—not the soft and easy times.

We need sometimes to learn to pray with Christina Rossetti:

God harden me against myself,
This coward with pathetic voice,
Who craves for ease and rest and joys.

SATURDAY—DECEMBER 18.

WHEN Lord Brabazon of Tara was 75 he set down some of the things which he said he had learned in his long, active and adventurous life. One of them was this: " If you can train yourself not to worry, you will have done more for yourself than any doctor can do for you. The unpleasant things in my life have always happened out of the blue. Meetings and other events I have dreaded and feared like the plague, have turned out to be not so bad. Do not hide today's sun therefore behind tomorrow's clouds."

SUNDAY—DECEMBER 19.

AND Mary shall bring forth a son, and thou shalt call his name Jesus: for he shall save his people from their sins.

THE JOURNEY

Life is a river
That slowly grows
And gathers strength
As it onward flows
By steep and valley, hill and lea
To find at last the eternal sea.

THE FRIENDSHIP BOOK

DICK SHEPPARD, who died in 1937, became famous while he was vicar of St Martin-in-the-Fields, London. During these years he was a frequent broadcaster and became known as the "Radio Parson". He came to be loved by countless listeners for his commonsense and humanity.

He once wrote down some words of Bismarck's which were typical of his approach to life: "When you want to take any fence in life, throw your heart over it first, and then your horse will follow."

YEARS ago Dobson and Young delighted thousands of listeners with their radio lecture-recitals on the piano. There was perfect harmony and understanding between them, but Dobson once let an interviewer into a secret:

"When we are on a lecture tour and have a day to spare, we get away from one another. He goes off fishing and I go walking, or do a spot of sketching. When we meet in the evening you might hear Young describing, not a big fish, but a kingfisher which perched on his rod and mistook him for a tree! And when he wants to see what I've painted I should probably admit that the view was so lovely that I just sat and looked at it."

We may be grateful indeed if we have experience of the kind of harmony and friendship which Dobson and Young enjoyed, but for us, as for them, there is a very real need for solitude, too, for times when we don't need to reproach ourselves for "doing nothing". Such moments fit us to face again the demands and pressure of life.

WEDNESDAY—DECEMBER 22.

I THINK you may find a smile in this notice that appeared in a Church news sheet:

" The Woman's Guild jumble sale will be held on the first Saturday of next month.

" As anything sellable would be gratefully received, would the ladies of the congregation cast their eyes round their households for objects they no longer wish to keep but could sell rather than throw out.

" Don't forget to bring your husbands."

THURSDAY—DECEMBER 23.

THE Sunday School teacher was telling her class about the birth of the Baby Jesus. When she came to the bit about there being no room at the inn, one boy shot up his hand and said, " Well, I blame Joseph, Miss. He should have booked!"

FRIDAY—DECEMBER 24.

ROAST the turkey,
Decorate the tree;
Jesus born in Bethlehem,
Joy for you and me.

Trudge the winter's snow,
Merry carols sing;
Jesus born in Bethlehem,
God's little Saviour King.

Bitterness and strife,
This world must cast away;
Jesus born in Bethlehem
This happy Christmas Day.

SATURDAY—DECEMBER 25.

NOW here's to you and here's to yours—
Good luck, good health, good cheer!
Unbroken may the circle be
This day and time next year.
May you abound in blessings,
May fortune favour you,
And if your way be hard, may God
Give strength to battle through.

SUNDAY—DECEMBER 26.

WHEN they saw the star, they rejoiced with exceeding great joy.

And when they were come into the house, they saw the young child with Mary his mother, and fell down, and worshipped him: and when they had opened their treasures, they presented unto him gifts; gold and frankincense, and myrrh.

MONDAY—DECEMBER 27.

OF the many lovely Christmas legends, one of my favourites is about the humble spider. The story goes that when Mary and Joseph were fleeing to Egypt with the newborn baby Jesus, they were pursued by soldiers and sought safety in a cave in the hillside.

A spider noticed their plight, and to make the place a little warmer for them, he spun a thick web over the opening to the cave. The soldiers saw the web and hurried past, and so the little family were spared.

Is this, I wonder, why some people feel superstitious about spiders, and will not harm them, calling them " lucky "?

AT EVE

Evening draws to a peaceful close,
  Time to wend our homeward way,
Secure that after a night's repose
  We'll wake to another bright new day.

TUESDAY—DECEMBER 28.

SEEK a friend in sunshine,
Show them that you care.
Seek a friend in shadows,
You'll be twice-blessed there.

WEDNESDAY—DECEMBER 29.

MILLIONS have found delight in the brilliant and sensitive music of James Galway, the flute-player. (" I am not a flautist," he once said. " I don't flaut and I have never possessed a flaut in my life!") That's another quality which has endeared him to multitudes—his humour.

But above all it is his courage in adversity that we must admire. Once, after playing at a concert in Switzerland, he was walking with friends to a restaurant just down the road.

Hearing the roar of an approaching motor-cycle, they drew into the side of the road, but it was to no avail. Three of them, including James Galway, were seriously injured and taken to hospital. Galway had both legs and an arm broken.

Three months passed and James Galway was still waiting to be allowed home. The bones were not knitting properly and it was a long time till eventually, in his wheelchair, he was able to play in public again.

His reaction to the accident speaks volumes for his philosophy of life: " I decided that henceforward I would play every concert, cut every record, give every TV performance as if it were my last. The important thing is to make sure that every time I play the flute my performance will be as near perfection as God intended and that I shall not be remembered for a shoddy performance."

IT has been said, " God gave us a sense of humour to prevent us from going mad." Certainly the ability to laugh at ourselves sometimes can save us a good deal of unnecessary frustration, anger and impatience . . . indeed, also groundless fear. We laugh at the small boys who were scared off by a notice which a gardener put at his gate to discourage them from searching for lost balls among his plants. It read: " Beware of the Hydrangea!"

But might we not laugh away some of our own fears if we tried? Surely Patrick Campbell did this when he wrote humorously about his fear of flying—how he always had an almost irresistible impulse to approach the captain before the flight and ask whether he or any of his forebears had been subject to fits of giddiness or to heart attacks! Then when the plane was in the air he was appalled to see the pilot coming down the aisle, " leaving some inexperienced boy in charge of the controls." It was even worse a few minutes later when he saw the pilot returning—carrying a screwdriver!

Things are not half as bad if we can learn to laugh at life. Even the gloomy headlines of the newspaper can often be lightened for us if we glance first at the cartoon. As the old proverb says, " A merry heart doeth good like a medicine."

LOOK for tomorrow, when today
Seems more than you can bear.
The sun is now behind the clouds,
Seek out the brightness there!

Where the Photographs were taken

A VILLAGE SPRING — *Astbury, Cheshire.*

LITTLE WORLD — *Oban, Argyll.*

THANK YOU — *Eastnor, Herefordshire.*

DREAMING — *Berriedale, Caithness.*

GIVING THANKS — *Conway Valley, Denbigh/ Carnarvonshire.*

NO HURRY — *High Ham, Somerset.*

BEST OF ALL — *Fowey, Cornwall.*

JUST WAIT — *Cwmyoy, Monmouthshire.*

GRAND DESIGN — *Glen Lyon, Perthshire.*

MEMORY — *Beddgelert, Carnarvonshire/Merioneth.*

ESCAPE — *Eilean Donan Castle, Dornie, Ross and Cromarty.*

VARIETY — *People's Park, Halifax, Yorkshire.*

IDEAL — *Watendlath, Cumberland.*

THE CROSSING — *Bolton Abbey, Wharfedale, Yorkshire.*

THE JOURNEY — *Kinnoull Hill, River Tay, Perth.*

AT EVE — *Arnside, Westmorland.*

Printed and Published by D. C. Thomson & Co., Ltd.,
185 Fleet Street, London EC4A 2HS.

© D. C. Thomson & Co., Ltd., 1981.

ISBN 0 85116 222 3